THE
100 DAY
WIFE

Our journey through the last weeks of life

Heike Rentel-Thomas

To the other half of Us – Everton Thomas

CONTENTS

ACKNOWLEDGEMENTS

I would like to thank my wonderful friends Mick, Jen, Sherri, Kelly, Leona, Wendy, Dawn, Jo, and Aly for keeping me alive to write these words. Thank you, Stephen, for the daily phone calls from Germany to check on me. And, of course, a big thank you to Sara (without an H) for the hours spent proofreading with and for me and her unwavering support. Thank you also to my sister Birgit, who somehow managed to give us medical advice without ever seeing the patient. None of this would have been possible without the wonderful support from St. Barnabas and our special nurse Aly, or indeed any of the medical team who surrounded us with all the possible care and expertise they could possibly give. There were many people who supported us and I am grateful and glad that I had the chance to meet the 'Liberty family' and that my Emperor could realise just how important he was to so many.

ABOUT THE AUTHOR

Heike Rentel-Thomas was born in Germany, grew up in Hamburg, and came to the UK in 1988. After working as a freelance translator, she qualified as a teacher and specialized in working with troubled young people who are unable to attend mainstream education. She moved to the south coast in 2013 to embark on further studies and embrace the life by the sea.

PREFACE

When two worlds collide so beautifully, so gracefully, when you find the one, the twin flame, the sole purpose for your existence, you hold on. In August 2019, I found him, he found me. We became Us. Two lost souls, two odd socks, we became Us, complete. And our future began. Life became shiny and we each had a purpose. So easily did this happen, we slipped into our ever after. I had only 18 months. We had only 18 months. 100 days of being your wife. 49 days of battling the nothing that would ultimately leave me with nothing. Without you and only this story to tell. I am writing this as a legacy to you, my love.

My complicated, beautiful, multi-faceted contradiction of a husband. Cancer, terminal. Two stark words. Words that held little meaning until they did. Our battle, our battle through the diagnoses that was 'nothing'. Your pain, our pain. The layers which needed to be exorcised before you could leave were a journey. A savage and surprising journey of memory, lucid dreams, loss, and resentments. Your family by your bedside, bringing love with a payoff of years of grief.

Let me walk you through our story. The story of 49 days in a new land, a new universe – end-of-life care with an inevitable outcome. Interwoven with the backstory of your life, complicated by wrong turns, toxic family relationships, failures and triumphs; a life you considered to be merely an existence, dominated by loneliness and searching for purpose and love. Neither of us knew, or even suspected, that the cancer had already started to take decisions out of our hands and that we would have to take your final journey together. This biographical account tries to make sense of your diagnosis, the medical care needed, the short time we had to understand what was happening to us, whilst simultaneously trying to navigate your past in the shape of resentment and a tightly woven net of neglect, hurt, and the search for redemption. It is an honest account of our attempts to keep dignity and love as well as finding some quality in what little time was left for us. It also is a memorial to you and your courage, strength, wisdom, and most of all your resilience. From being a new husband, you grew into a mischievous Don, but, in the end, I had to let you go and fly away on a gust of wind. Our journey towards your death might be familiar to some and yet to be experienced by others. As well as trying to capture my beautiful husband, I have attempted to describe the last days of a man's life, the quality that can be retained and the beauty in every last moment, however short the time might be. Nothing was difficult whilst we were together, but the 'After' is maybe the topic for another book. This account has been written during the first ten days after your death and if it feels breathless and haunted then it encapsulates the emotions during that period.

1

Lilac Paper Curtains

Lilac paper curtains, designed to soften the assault on the senses. Folded in precise patterns, sharp corners. Speckled blue floor, spotlessly clean, rounded edges for easy cleaning. Bright lights, too bright, eyes hurting. My eyes fixed on the monitor above your head. BP, oxygen, pulse. The beeping is irregular, far too fast. Your eyes are fixed on me, I smile. What else is there to do, apart from watching and smiling and hoping that everything will be ok? I hold your hand, tightly, trying not to transmit what I am thinking. If I am thinking anything. Is there thought? Your skin is warm, your grip strong. I remember another adventure. Not long ago. They closed the road to the station, you had worked longer than you thought and I could not get to the station to meet you, so I drove through the woods until I got as close as I could. Parked behind a tarmacking van with bright yellow lights. A friendly road worker enquired about my wellbeing. I called you, gave you directions, but you always had trouble finding your way. You come out of the station, turn left, and you see me behind the yellow lights. I waited for a long time and still did not see you. Your sauntering, sliding way of moving forward, as if gliding on air cushions that nobody could see. I called you again, you had walked in the wrong direction, maybe half a mile away from the sea. I told you to walk back to the station and I would meet you there. Hated the thought of you being lost in the dark in a place you did not know; tired, hungry, just wanting to be at home. Walking towards the station was exhilarating, the evening was still warm and walking in the middle of a normally busy main road was somehow fitting. Tarmac smells, reminiscent of hell or the dungeons in Venice rose from the fresh road surfaces. When I saw you, I skipped a bit, right in the middle of the road, right where nobody can walk. You did not speed up, but you sauntered a little more purposefully. The bottle in your pocket. I hoped that it was whiskey, not vodka – vodka meant you were sad. We met halfway between the station and the car, or the car and the station, depending on where you started from, nevertheless – halfway. Glad. The friendly road worker smiled and was glad that I had found you. I took a wrong turn in the woods, not knowing which way we should go. Utterly dark now, only our headlights and trees. I must have taken these roads hundreds of times before, never in the dark though and felt completely at sea. But we were together, and nothing bad could happen, it might just all take a little longer than planned. You sipped from the bottle, brown liquid, not vodka, so I knew things were not too bad. Trees, trees, and more trees in the dark. I had a general sense of direction, but no idea where to go, so just following the road was the best option. We drove all the way through Angmering estate. Warning signs about keeping out and private roads but turning was not an option. We had an adventure. Maybe we were lost, maybe we were just driving in the wrong direction. But it did not matter. We hit the main road home. Laughing. Not quite where I had expected to come out, but ok, familiar. On our way home. Home, where you were safe, and I was happy.

I am telling you about that day. You smile, the monitor still beeping and showing your racing pulse. The noises from the other curtained rooms annoy you. You want to go home. Patience is not one of your strong traits. I read in your face, the woman in the bed opposite reminds you of your mother – early dementia stages. I squeeze your hand. We will go home soon. We are waiting for someone to talk to us. Waiting and watching the little red numbers, breathing with the beat of the monitor. You are hungry, I need a coffee. You squeeze my hand 'go on, find something.' The hospital's Costa has closed a little while ago, but the shop is still open. A big box of Jaffa cakes. Before you, I did not know that I might like them – I still don't, to be honest, but they are easy to eat and remind you of some good bits of childhood. Back down the corridor where you collapsed. I try not to remember. Marching on, confusing rabbit hole of corridors. But I make my way back. You are not in our curtained room. The bed is gone, the monitor silent. But your shoes are neatly placed under my chair. So, deep breath, they would not have taken the care to arrange the shoes if something serious had happened. Be rational. Don't panic.

Sitting, with my feet on the blue floor, listening to the man behind the next curtain. He had fallen over, nothing to do with the drink in him at all, he says. I can feel the nurse smile resignedly. Looking at my shoes, I am suddenly cold, so very cold. Without the little red numbers there is nothing to fix my eyes to. Nothing to hold me together. They had become my horizon, my fixed point and without your input they are silent. Just a flickering screen. I stare at the Jaffa cakes, not sure where to put them. 'Put' is a strange word, not stand, lay, lean, or place in any particular way; abandon, put aside, things without a place. Blue box, too big and awkward to just keep on my lap. Reading the writing on the side of the box, not sure that I am taking any of it in. Not sure that I could recite the nutritional values of a Jaffa cake, per 100 gr. or portion. Suddenly, I feel hot, far too hot. Too many bright lights. Your bed, coming back, you turn the corner, looking more drained than ever. You had a CT scan. It is five o'clock in the afternoon. Your skin looks grey, your eyes bright, you hold my hand again. I tell you about your shoes and how they reassured me. You smile and say that you were worried that I might be worried. Too many worries about each other. I put my head next to yours and you sigh. The scan procedure tired you out. We share the Jaffa cakes with the nurse. He is compassionate, human – making conversation about nothing in particular.

We all raise an eyebrow at the man who fell over because his feet were not working, which had nothing to do with the drink. I think back to my recent research. A little bit of my liver, if I am suitable, can make it all ok. Your thoughts are drifting, I can see. Not sure where they are, but they are fast, racing thoughts. They show on the monitor. I stroke you shoulder, your chin, your cheek. Come back. We are just waiting, nothing really bad is going to happen. This is the 21st century after all. We have come a long way in medicine, nothing that cannot be fixed. There is a solution, there will be a way forward. Just waiting for the doctor. He will finish his clinic at 6.30. He will come to see us, and we will write a roadmap. Your thoughts are back in the room, you want to go home. Ranting a bit about doctors, time keeping, and overinflated sense of importance. I give you a Jaffa cake, you smile. You don't really want to eat it, but it passes the time. The nurses fix another drip. It took them a long time to find a vein and your skin is already turning blue where they tried to take blood. I am trying to remember the difference between veins and arteries but talk about dinner instead. Maybe a takeaway? I have made soup. Your mouth twitches, trying a smile that is not really there. Maybe I take tomorrow off work, and we can go for a walk. One of the nurses has lost the patient who fell over and is now wandering around with a gashing head wound, which is categorically not due to drink, but bleeds nevertheless. Your breath and pulse are still too fast and tacky. The little red numbers show me how the drip is doing the work of bringing your blood pressure back. I am happy. Bit of fluid and you are ok. You will be ok – we will be ok. Is the car close enough for you to walk to? I am playing with the ring on your little finger. A worry ring. We found it in Arundel whilst looking for engagement rings. The last shop we looked. You always wanted a Celtic ring, and the moving middle part was an absolute bonus. That day was a good day. It had been drizzly all day, but you were determined to find rings for us. There had been a strange sense of urgency in you. It had to be that day and no other. We wanted to find old rings, the right ones. In the large conversion full of little antique places, we found what we were looking for. Simple and silver. It was too small for your ring finger, so it is sitting snugly on your little one. I turn the middle and you hold my face.

Your heartbeat is strong, slower – we will be just fine. A blip, a turn because of the stress of coming here. Nothing to worry about. We know that the news is not going to be great, but we are prepared. We both have theories … yours is the lung, mine the liver. We have talked about it, our worst fears, yours and mine. They were not the same. They found the man with the headwound. The lady opposite moans softly, she does not know where she is. Frightened, alone and in pain. Your feet are getting restless. I hope the doctor comes soon, before you get too frustrated. You can be unpredictable when you have to wait. Nobody is important enough for you to wait for them. Apart from the last, straddling van driver at the warehouse, or the bin people on a Friday when you have to lock up. The thin blue blanket keeps sliding off your knees. I put it back. Not enough pillows for sure. Remembering another day. The first day, which was not a day, but a night. Fate and destiny. The 20th of September, just about, because it was 02.30. We had not met yet, but inescapably, as if guided by runners or tracks, we were moving towards each other. Setting in motion a whole new life, a whole new future. My thoughts interrupted by an opening of the curtain wall. A handsome young man with doe eyes and a small nurse with a solemn expression.

I straighten my back, put by feet back on the floor. You look at me, a split second of understanding and then at these two people, who are holding our future in their hands. Not their hands, but their words. The words that must surely come. They introduce themselves, names, I am sure, lost in my ears, not arriving anywhere. I stare at the nurse's eyes, and I know. I just know. My toes shake, blank, empty, surrounded by lilac – breathe. First the questions. How long have you been feeling like this? Do you drink? How much? A few months – 40 + years – at least a bottle a day – mainly spirits, mixed in with wine. You grip my hand; I shift from the nurse to the doctor. His mouth moving – that explains what the scan showed. I will him to hurry and I will him to not say anything, I want to hear, and I want him to go away. You stare at him, gripping me tighter. His words stay stuck in the air, suspended, foreign – lesions, tumour, blisters, no viable tissue, metastasised. I can see the words, hovering around the room, clustering, clotting, trying to catch them and put them back. And yet; you nod. That is all you do – you nod. I shift my eyes to the nurse. 'Transplant?' she shakes her head; I can see she is welling up. She must be used to this, surely. Why the tears? 'Nothing,' the doctor is sad. 'More tests?' 'Nothing,' he says. 'Nothing' is a big word at a time when I can only understand small ones. You nod again. 'How long?' Your face is stoic, straight, without expression, but your fingers are making my hand bleed. Our brains merge into one, empty space with just 'Nothing' in it. And then 'Nothing' is joined by 'two weeks, maybe four'. Weeks … Weeks … how long is a week? 7 days … 14 days … maybe 28 days. Days are shorter than weeks and weeks are shorter than months. Whatever happened to fabric curtains? We married seven weeks ago … 51 days. We nod, as one. You thank them, I thank them. My eyes lock into the nurse's gaze. 'Nothing,' she shakes her head. You straighten your back, loosen your grip. We are going home. No need to stay here. No need to say anything. Waiting for the paperwork; discharge papers. They will ring on Monday. We will make plans. Plans for what? Plans for 28 days? We have made plans for 20 years. Retirement, travel, reading, writing, work, plans. How can we now make plans for 28 days – at the most – maybe we have to fit 28 days into 14. It will take that long to understand. Days, weeks, not months, not years, not a lifetime. Or a lifetime in 28 days.

We are numb, our bodies and minds are one, melted together, fused by 'Nothing' and 'Weeks'. I stare at my phone, trying to see the time. I want to remember this moment. I need to remember. Our hands are not shaking, we are not crying, we are not anything, we are 'Nothing', 'Weeks'. We are tumours, lesions, things growing that should not be there, invaders, invited by you a long time ago, your ultimate way of hurting yourself, as always directing your own movie. I help you dress. You ask where the toilets are, I don't know. I find the nurse who has been looking after us. He takes you in the right direction. You move slowly, deliberately, not sauntering, not sliding, shuffling, one foot in front of the other. I watch, stare; you walking away, me sitting here with the Jaffa cakes. The nurse returns, he takes my arm, he is sorry. His eyes tell me that he is sincere. He is sincerely sorry. He feels what we feel. But he will stay here, with the lilac curtains, and help to fix people. We cannot be fixed. Unfixable; beyond repair; nothing to be done; going home for days, the same number of days as your annual leave, but fewer than we have been married. You are getting impatient, needing a cigarette, air. Needing to get away from this room, the now pointless bleeping and flashing numbers. They are there for people who get better, who go home for years. I help you up, gather our things, unsure what to do with the Jaffa cakes and just leave them on the bed. Someone says that they will call the next day. We nod. You hold onto me. We move towards the doors. We walk through the green waiting room, full of people, impatiently waiting for someone to fix, heal, plaster, glue, administer health. I look at them. I look at your feet. Shuffling – you don't shuffle … you glide. Please glide, please saunter. My arm supports your weight. The car is not too far away. You roll a cigarette, staring ahead. We are going home. After so many hours, we are going home. With 'Nothing' and metastasis and 'weeks'.

'I am not going back into hospital', your voice in the dark. We hold hands and I steer with one arm. It was never in question; you need to be home. The first home you have ever had, ever wanted. Your statement hangs in the air, becomes ours, becomes us. Defines us from now on. The road is familiar, no thinking required, your profile drawn by streetlights onto the canvas of the dark car. No question – no hospitals, no drips or poking. Enough poking. No more not knowing, speculating, researching, talking, exploring possibilities.

You sigh. My phone rings. Your daughter. Not sure what to say. You take my phone, answer. You tell her what I have not completely understood yet. You use words I have to get used to, there is no time for me to collect my thoughts. You are saying the words as if they mean nothing. They mean everything, change everything. I need to collect us, put us together, before I can use any words. You are not brave, you are empty. Our world sits behind frosted glass, bubbled, suffocating in 'Nothing'. And so, we arrive home. Not sad, not angry, not brave, we just arrive home.

2

Kidneys

We talk through the night, tired, hollow eyed, staring down the one-way road someone has placed in front of us, without the option to refuse entry or bolt. We talk about what we can bear and what would be impossible. We talk about the 'Nothing' and try to find 'Something'. We talk about getting stronger and 'Maybe'. Your face looks like always, maybe a little tired, maybe drawn, but the smooth skin has room for the roundness of your cheeks. We are holding each other for hours, drawing deeper and deeper into the 'Us'. Fighting talk followed by acceptance. Endless visits at Google, finding ways, looking for something that is other than 'Nothing'. Something, anything that could buy us time. The hydrangea in front of the window sways in the wind. First light; the flat attracts a special light in the mornings. I make coffee and we lean back, watching the light hitting the sides of the walls outside. The light wanders, the hydrangea sways and the seagulls cry into the upcoming storm. 18 months ago, their cries disturbed you, like the spray from the angry sea. Now you smile, watching the light, watching me and grow wistful. Bits are breaking in me, not sure if you can hear them; 'Don't leave me ... take me with you.' You turn onto my pillow, 'They don't know everything; we will have years. I decide when I go.' I cannot contradict you; I want to believe, I am holding onto your words like a fish to the hook. Holding onto us. Not hope, just us. We are strong, together we are unbeatable. We have conquered everything in our path. Us, We, as One.

We talk about the kidnap, 18 months ago. When I came to the airport, before I could recognise your smell, could feel your skin from any distance. You flew in from a holiday, Gatwick, not that far from me. I had misunderstood. You had said you would arrive Saturday at 12.30. I thought it to be in the afternoon, but it was 12.30 at night, Friday night. Definitions are crucial sometimes, and sometimes it makes no difference. I had told you about my guestroom and that I would meet you at the airport. Your flight was delayed by hours, I kept an eye on the ticker on the laptop at home, telling you about your schedule, before you knew it yourself. We arrived at the same time, maybe five minutes apart, 02.30. I parked, walked across to the smoking area in front of the North Terminal. Not nervous, not questioning, not wondering about anything, apart from maybe not recognising you. You later said that you wondered 'who does THAT?' We did that. Us. As we became Us. You looked at me, took my shoulders, held me for a minute and we walked to the car, talking, forging Us. Winding into each other to become one being. Talking. Your eyes looked blue in the moonlight. You had cataracts, but I did not know that then. You laughed at my love for pillows. Only later, during the pandemic, did you appreciate their presence, their softness, their warmth. You marvelled at my cottage, my hidden place, the place just for me. The place where nobody was welcome, my own rabbit hole. And you stayed until Sunday night. My heart boarded the train with you, your heart attached itself to the pillows, the cat, and the books. I lived off your smell for a whole week. Your smell and very little else.

Your leg settles against mine; we look at each other. Nothing feels like 28 days, or 14 or days at all. Normal, coffee, the wind, the light, not sad yet, we do not hear the thing in you growing. It is silent. No pain. Silently growing and weaving around your cells. After the coffee and snippets of news, you make some calls and I set off. Normal, like on every other day since you fell ill. You in bed, me on my travels. Messages, checking, assuring each other, bridging the need to be One.

The nurse calls as I am leaving the carpark. I pull over. She tried to ring your number but could not get through. Little mercies. We talk about the 'Nothing', the 28 days, the 14 days, we talk about you getting stronger, maybe 'Nothing' might change. She tells me that she has referred us to a hospice. A new word, not new, but new to us. A concept I had not thought about, that had not entered my mind. She must feel my raised eyebrows. No, she assures me, not for going to. For coming to us. A nurse, visiting, supporting, providing. I am glad that she did not talk to you first. You would have stopped listening after the word. I catch my breath. Hospice. That is where people die. Where people care for people who die. Where they have geraniums and pretend it is home. Normal. A new shade of normal surrounds me. I want more than weeks, I need months. On the way into the supermarket, I forget my mask. I must not forget your lottery ticket. I hate lottery tickets, informed you of the statistical, mathematical odds and you laughed – and I am getting three lucky dips. Because we are lucky, normal, coffee and wind and hydrangeas in the front garden. You are not dying, you are strong. The thing growing in you cannot do what they say it will.

The cat meets me at the door, hungry, always hungry. You are in bed, smiling. 'We will have visitors,' you say. I am unsure about the plural. We have been selective, careful, introducing only a few into this space. Our safe space, home, your home, my home, our home. You had made sure that nobody knew where we were. Nobody from that other life of yours, the one before Us. I smile, make a coffee, and start my research. On food, drugs, alternatives, herbals, treatments, options, alkaline food, and healing crystals. Anything short of chanting. You hold my face, radiant, determined. I tell you about the call and that we will get another call shortly. Hospice. Your face falls, you let go of me. I explain and you breathe.

No problem, we will talk and see what they offer. Support? Why do we need support? We are ok, normal. Nothing has changed since the day before yesterday. You are serious now.

No quips, no glint in your eye. Your thoughts are going to a place that I cannot follow. I make more coffee. The lunchtime light breaks through the window, disturbing some dust on the pictures we bought on our journey to us. Suddenly I cannot see my future self. Lost. Where have I gone? Where have you gone? The hospice will be in touch on Monday to make arrangements. Arrangements for what? What are they expecting to happen? What can we not see? I turn to you. You are tired, your two-week stubble irritates you. I lay next to you and cradle your head. Soft snoring. You stir in your sleep as I move to the laptop. Finding out, understanding, is key. Liver, what does the liver do? Why does it break? Your face, beautiful and serene, rests on my shoulder. I stay still, try to read rather than type. My mind wanders back. There were signs: many, small, infinitesimal, but there were signs. I missed them. Maybe you did, too. The forgetfulness, the little blue pills, the itching – I should have known, should have tried to make you do something. You turn slightly, breathing softly and strong. Tired, but normal. Your phone shrills. The dust seems to shriek, all noise amplified in the silence. You startle, answer, smile. 'And so it begins.' Married 52 days ago. The doorbell rings. Answering, up the stairs from the basement, three men, nephews, your brother's sons. Noisy, one with a stutter. They mumble their names, well mannered, leaving their shoes at the door. Big men, loud, bearing fish and chips because this is the coast. Suddenly the room feels small, too small for all these bodies. And you appear smaller than you did before I opened the door. Smaller, but harder. You speak differently, strange. As if in a foreign language. You laugh and I make coffee that nobody wants. They brought beer.

Your brother's sons. They are grateful to you. The ultimate debt. Four years ago, you gave their father life. Your brother, sickle cell damaged, needed a kidney. And you gave it, without asking or waiting or any doubt. I know that you had lied to the surgeon. You had told her that you took a drink from time to time. Only during the operation did she realise that you had an affinity with alcohol that surpassed anything else. You had a super kidney, more valves than usual. Perfect for both of you. Perfect for saving a life.

The life of a brother who had shared your hell. Who had been one of the gang of three, who were looking after the others, stealing, cheating, ducking, diving – looking after the young ones whilst your mother was locked away in some faraway place. Fragile mother, deeply loved, absent, unresponsive, and leaving the young ones in the older one's care. Your brother's boys, who had buried their mother six months ago. You – their uncle – elder statesman, with one kidney, lying in bed, holding court. Fighting talk that is new. Harsher, determined. The air tingles under the strain of your positivity. Suddenly you look well. Talk about people and times and events, laugh, try some fish. Good, fish is good for you, fish oil makes people stronger. I look closer. Your eyes say different. You are in pain, you wince when you move, but not so that anyone sees. You laugh, but your eyes don't follow your lips. I stand in the doorway, holding my coffee, thinking about polite men, who leave their shoes at the door, who are mourning their mother and came all the way to see the man who saved their father. I smile at you, and you wink. Unbroken bond, Us, We, the show of a fighter, of a winner with a chink in his armour. Invisible, growing inside you. I can see that you are slowly, reluctantly, working your way through the fish. Spreading batter around the paper, pushing fish under chips, trying to will the food away. I sit in the kitchen with the cat for a while, hoping nobody is going to report the visit. Lockdown is still in full swing. If lockdowns and swing are not directly opposing ideas. I contemplate this for a moment, dismiss the thought and join you again.

The smell of the fish and the oil seeps into the walls. I want to open the window but would have to move nephews out of the way. So, I don't, just sit next to you on the bed. Our bed, our most sanctuous place. Unspoiled, untouched, the place where we talk, where you teach me about the boy, lost inside you. I am an aunt to three strapping young men. Somehow, I find this amusing. You look at me giggle and smile. It is late and grows later, but we sit and you talk. After they leave, hugging me, strange contact with strangers and thanking me for looking after you, I return to the room. You are wistful, tired, look worn. I open the window. A gust of cold air streams into the room; makes you shiver. I pull the covers up over your shoulders and we look at each other. 'There will be more', you say, 'but it will pass. They all have to come; they have to see. And then they will no longer come until the end.' I kiss you, knowing the sacrifice you are willing to make. Following some law of clan and kinship I don't understand. 'Too much?' you ask, and I shake my head. I have not been an aunt to strangers before and they are respectful and grateful. I try not to look into your eyes, avoiding gazes that could read my confusion. I busy myself, taking beer cans and paper into the kitchen, straighten the carpets and make another coffee. Tea for you tonight, turmeric tea, I read that it cures many things.

Settling next to you again, I find a chip under my pillow. You stretch out your arm for me to nest. My hand rests on your stomach, towards the right, just under the rib cage. And we talk about the kidney and the warnings the surgeon gave you. About your brother, who was not well enough to come with his sons today. About you nicking and ducking and diving. We do not talk tonight about the thing growing in you. Maybe if we forget, it might forget as well.

3

Not Enough Chairs

The night is long, you struggle. Somehow, your breathing has changed. Faster, shallow, laboured, as if excited after a long run. We talk about Anton. He is not well, your brother with your kidney, he is not well at all. You tell me about his achievements, proud, you are so immensely proud of your martial art brother. A master no less. Dedicated to his art, his way of thinking. You, who always called himself the biggest failure of all, are proud of this man; your brother, father to three polite young men, carrier of your kidney. You are proud and I am proud. We are married 53 days. We talk about going to London one day, meeting your brother. You think we would have a lot to talk about. The art of thinking. You want a wooden man. I will find one. The morning is grey, unremarkable, with the promise of rain. I welcome rain, it makes being warm precious. My head on your shoulder as you speak. I can feel your chest moving in tune with the words. 'There will be people,' you say, 'many people'. I rest my leg on yours – if they love you, I will love them. You have made public statements. Modern world statements, Facebook, WhatsApp – telling the world about the silent thing in you. I am not ready for statements. I need to be silent, quiet, finding words that are not pompous, not loud in their screams for attention. Are they my statements to make anyway? How do you describe the broken, the normal, the Nothing, the hospice – without self-importance, indulgent self-pity, and yet enough weight to convey the upcoming pain? Your leg is warm against mine. The cat, confused by the new hours we keep, shouts for food. I go and make coffee. You no longer want it black, still with three sugars. Sugar is good. Sugar spells calories. You have never been an eater. Calories came from the bottle. Empty calories we can no longer afford. The coffee is warm and bitter, the cat is fed. There must be someone, someone I know who can help. Someone who knows what to do. I know people who plumb, wire, compose, fix engines and carpets, people who fix brains and paint pictures of the inside of heads. I don't know anyone who fixes the Nothing. I boil an egg for you. Protein. A building block – essential. Please eat your egg. You smile like a child and indulge me. Propped up in the pillows, checking your phone, revelling in messages of support. Fighting talk. Can we beat this? The odds are uneven. Unfair to the visible soldier. Scales in favour of the invisible one. Not invisible on the pictures, the scans. Visible to the doctor's hands. I place my hand back on the spot under your ribs, you stroke my hair. I cannot feel it and yet I should know. Can unreality hit? I know reality can. The world appears to be wrapped in a cloudy film. I kiss you and take the plate. Visitors. There will be visitors. Later. For now, Us, We, are intact, undisturbed, smiling.

Unsteady, you make your way to the bathroom. I stand back, watching, ready to jump – to catch you. But you succeed. Breathing a sigh of relief, Us, We have mastered a hurdle. Walking a small distance, like climbing a mountain without air. But you did not need my arm this time.

You don't know that I busy myself near you, so that the arm is ready. At least I hope you don't know. You settle back under the covers; I check milk and coffee and tea. We have cups. In my other life, years ago, before the cottage, I needed cups, plenty of cups. The world came to me. I welcomed the world in the same way, in which I now welcome the silence. It was a big world, music, plenty of music and cake. I smile. You don't like cake. Since the operation, you say, you don't like cake. A shame – I am a better baker than cook. And without the world in my house and you not liking cake, I have not baked in a long time. The doorbell hums in its shrill demand. I look at you, you wink. Two of your sons. The one with your name and a silent, forgotten one. Unsure of me, of themselves, of you. Taking them to you, we try to make conversation. We have never met, and yet, I lead them into our bedroom. I don't want them to notice that there are no pictures of them. Just my children. You defended our walls against them. Polite, awkward young men. Sitting on chairs I bring from the other room. Chairs that I bought when I came to the coast a long time ago. They have tea. I am searching their faces for you. No trace. They are your sons, but out in the world, I would not have known who they are. Space, I need to give them space. They have not seen you in a long time. You kept them away. On my way to the kitchen, I scan their faces. You told me about the one with your name. You think him weak.

And yet, many years ago, he stood up to you. And it pained you to tell me. That day, when you returned from somewhere, after a long time of absence, and he told you to leave. He, all 14 years of him, was now the man of the house. You had left them, just as your mother used to, to fend for themselves. Good intentions. Protection you said. From what remained unsaid. Best endeavours. You left them in a hostile world. Absent even when present. At the bookies or in Bristol, unattainable either way. Betting or doing business, always bearing gifts or staying away. The son with your name needed your presence, your love. You could not give it. You tried; I am sure. Now he does not need it anymore. Maybe approval, but you cannot give that, because you don't feel it. You think him weak. And yet, watching your face from the door, I can see that you need him. Need him to be your son, where you could not be his father. Wash cups, do something. Something is always better than Nothing. And the doorbell again. More daughters, two this time, I know one of them.

She was at our wedding, the second witness. Fragile, unfelt bravado. Your youngest daughter, who was a son once. Trying too hard to be brave. But what is that really – brave? I need you to hold my hand. I am not brave. Too many faces. Noise, too much noise. Brave is facing things we understand. Brave is being afraid and staying. Fighting this thing is not brave. We cannot see it or win.

You are holding court. Kissing faces, letting their tears flow all over you. Soaking their pain into your skin. Granddaughter, second daughter, your children, my strangers. On my pillows, leaning against you. You smiling. You have not eaten. You wince when you move. There is pain. I am numb. You are not going, not yet; we are just finding a new normal, a new safe. Fortify home to make it safe for us. We, Us, as one. No space in the room. I walk into the kitchen. People in the kitchen, making tea. Milk. There is never enough milk. I should have cleaned the fridge. I meant to a week ago, but then I forgot. Strangers opening the cupboard, helpful, smiling. Someone is rolling a joint. I stand back in the door to our bedroom. Looking at you. You don't see me. Everyone is crying. They should make memories now, not tears. Another sister, elegant and arrogant. Seeping condescending helpfulness from her fur coat. It is not cold enough for fur coats. Seat at the window. I bring more chairs. Another daughter, your eldest. Complications, old wounds burst open in our kitchen. Spilling puss and wine all over the air and the cat. Brothers and sisters and yet cousins. Justifications, resentment, and expectations fermenting together into explosive toxins. Everyone is breathing them in. The cat looks sad. I look into the bedroom. The Don in his bed. All you need is a ring for them to kiss. With the arrival of the eldest daughter, the second daughter leaves the room. Sitting with me and her husband amongst my books. The room where we eat. Where we read or talk. Where we see friends. She sits with her husband. I am on the sofa, in the corner. Smaller, I must become smaller. They talk, friendly, loud, incomprehensively large hoop earrings dangling in the fading light.

Mouths moving, spitting words at me, friendly, loud words. Welcome to the family. A family of strangers. Yesterday I had three nephew strangers, now six children. The eldest is getting drunk in the kitchen. She stands before me and says, 'You are new'. I am not new. I am old. I have been here forever. I have been me for as long as I remember. She spills white wine over the counter. I mop it up. The youngest daughter steps in. Old bullets cloaked in words flying around the lampshades. Your eldest tells me that her mother is coming. Closure she says. Closure is needed. You have told me about them, the pain, the time spent defending yourself. I know everything, the past, the mistakes. But knowing and feeling are separate. I am cold, unspeakably cold.

No air, just toxin. People, in the bedroom, the kitchen, the living room. People talking and crying. I look into the room where you hold your court. Animated, excited, not normal, but well. I take my coat – run … I need to run. Always been a runner. With you, with us, for Us, for the One that we are, I let the running shoes go. I said I would stay, tender roots feeling their way into the warm earth of our souls. Staying. I promised to stay. Not flee from country to country. Stay and build a nest for Us. For the One that we have become. For your skin, your breath, the little one hidden inside you.

I run up the stairs. Leaving the basement, the nest, the bubble that can no longer protect me. Run to the beach. Sit and breathe. Breathe. Seagull air around me. Rain. Calling a friend, anyone. Someone who can hold me. Just for a minute, a second, hold me together.

Sarah is running down the promenade towards me. I am so cold; I cannot feel her touch on my shoulder. Screaming. My screams. I can hear them. They are mine as they mingle with the cold air and then become part of the bigger, the wider, the world. Suddenly, rain, sheet rain, puddles, cold rain on my hair. I am unspeakably tired. My bed, our bed. A blanket. The cat. I don't want a friend, I want you. We are running home, across the street, back into the building. A man opens the door, a stranger, large in every way. Tall, stocky, well built, assured and calm. Looking at me. I am the stranger. Breathless. Your brother, another brother. He smiles and welcomes me into our space. I shudder. Cups, empty cups on all tables, on chairs, on the floor. I try to find you. You look up. As if feeling my presence. Your face falls, darkening eyes. You follow me into the kitchen, stare at me. There is pity in your eyes. You touch my shoulder. Overwhelmed?' I stare back at you. I cannot feel you. 'Stand your ground, my Queen.' What ground would you like me to stand? The king is dying, and you want me to injure his children? Sarah makes conversation. I cannot remember names. 'Have they upset you?' What do you want me to say? I shake my head. My hands are red from the cold. I want to touch your face, your beautiful, haunted face, but the cold might hurt you. I help you back into the room. Everyone is staring. You are upright. No stoop, no shuffling. The Don. And his queen, but I don't want to be a queen. I want to be us. I want normal. I need normal. Now more than ever. 26 days of normal. Roots, tentatively growing, ripped out by one word: Nothing. Milestones, we need Milestones. We need points on the map. Holding on to dates. Not slip from 26 days to 12. The eldest has left her bottle of wine, empty. Anger, great anger. Does she not know? Does she not know what is killing you? How drowning the past has drowned our future? How can she not know? They left, they all left.

Darkness outside, wet, soggy, cold darkness. It is creeping into my bones through the window. Leaving the sheets clammy. *Danke* is a beautiful word, it means 'thank you' in German. I tell you and your face splits into a smile. I boil an egg for you and some rice. Brown rice is better than white. You are tired when I return into the room. Tired, sunken eyes, the smile still painted into your face. I burry my head under your arm, you kiss my hair. 'No worries, they do understand. You're just overwhelmed. It will pass.' Pleased that they will understand, we turn on the news and discuss cats, and the weather, and Egypt.

A text from your youngest, she has sent to your eldest. Berating, spitting hurt, angry letters exploding on the small screen. You sigh. You blame her. She has a temper. You don't know what was said. I tell you. I need to defend the youngest. So, what was to be secret, to be kept, for you to be protected from, spills from my lips. You close your eyes. Exhausted. I need to find things to make you stronger, calmer, happier, put weight on, because maybe, if you get stronger, calmer, happier, heavier, they might agree after all to more tests.

4

Pink Quartz

Our nights are getting worse. You cannot sleep. It might be the dark; it might be pain. I hold you in your fitful, uneasy sleep. Waking up to boxers on your small screen. You are watching it without break. We got married 54 days ago. You cradle my chin. Coffee, you made coffee. Spilled all over the floor, but that does not matter. You walked to the kitchen. Made coffee. A shadow creeps over your face. 'What happened last night?' I had feared that question. What can I say? The truth? All that pain in this space, all that anger. And I think back to that day in the cottage, when you told me the story of sisters and children and a boy, who could not make good. The boy, just out of prison, running scared with nowhere to go. A girl, both children, she ambitious, he lost. They had a daughter, gave her a name. He went legit, she stayed at home. Did you love her? You were not sure, maybe a bit. You were friends in a group from way back, school, neighbours for many years. All of them damaged. All of them alone. You tried to make a home, but really, you had no idea how. You worked, she cheated. Too young both and either of you. She wanted better, more. You worked harder. It was not enough. You caught her one night. Stayed downstairs until the morning. And then made breakfast and left. Back to your mother's house. Back to the other madness. She wanted money, you gave it to her, worked harder, living at your mother's house. 20 and 21. Back to thieving and ducking and diving, to provide for a child whom you felt you had failed before it even began. Your eldest daughter.

We discover that you can no longer walk without help. How can I hold you, support you without you noticing? You drink gallons of water – thirsty, always thirsty. Three days since the doctor with the doe eyes issued his sentence. Four days since you sauntered, maybe longer. Hindsight is blind. I cannot remember. I feel my cheeks, wet. I want to remember, I need to remember, but all I see is you in the hospital corridor, collapsing. No fretting, pointless use of my brain. We need to make plans, need to research. Increase our chances, that's what we need to do. Not dwell on things that are hidden or no longer of any relevance. My phone bleeps, a message. Your eldest daughter, having stayed at a B&B in our road, wants to see me. She has things to say. Apologies to make. Plenty of places to stay along our road. Opposite the beach. Tourists stay in the summer. Your eldest is staying in a four-poster bed to reclaim what she thinks is rightfully hers. We talk. I cannot decide on my own. I do not need any more children. I need to work on my understanding of the invisible thing. You do not need your past to haunt you, you need to get stronger, heavier, and calm.

So, I meet her. The rain has subsided. Just cold wind over the grass. The beach is invisible behind the incline of green. She talks. About her mother and feeling rejected. I wonder, does she know? Does she really know what happened? I am not going to tell her, easy as it would be.

Not my story to tell. Not for me to tell her how she was adopted against your will by the man who married her mother and went on to abuse, hidden and protected by her mother. And how everyone knew, except you. And yet, no time for platitudes either. So, I tell her – whatever she tries, she cannot and will not reclaim 40 years in 24 days. That time, however long, would not be enough. Like sleep, once it is lost, you cannot regain it. You cannot make up for insomnia by sleeping for days. Better to skip it. Insomnia is my friend. Has been for years. Better not sleeping than having dreams. But I do not tell her that. I say that her mother has hurt you and anyone who hurts you is not welcome in my house. She nods, seems grateful, sincere. I put my arms round her shoulders. A victim of your life, after all. We return together. I make tea, only to find her on my pillows, cradled into you. You are smiling at me, apologetic. I say nothing, she is your child. She will return every weekend, alone, not again with your fur-coated sister, who arrives later, with names of alternative healers. Money no object she says. More visitors, more blurry names and faces. Still loud, still crude in a loving way. Your face grows tighter, the dark patch under your eyes expanding to the top of your cheeks. Can they not see? Before she leaves, I ask your eldest to think. Whom is this for – you, her, or her mother? I know the answer, but she might not. Mid-afternoon and the first chair breaks. Not used to being carried, just used to standing there and us sitting on them. I will remember to find the glue and the nails. Every visit to the bathroom is now a public display. I do not want anybody's eyes on you, on your increasingly skinny legs. When nobody is looking, you squeeze my hand. There is pain. The doctor has given us morphine, to tide us over, but you refuse it – for now. You want to know where the pain is, as if it makes the thing visible. I stroke your neck. We make our way back to the room, the party of mourners with nothing to mourn – yet. Late afternoon and they are beginning to leave. They have work in the morning and it is a long journey. After I close the door behind the last stranger, I can still see their prints on the floor, their breath in the curtains and their hair on my pillow. You snore softly. A hard day for you. I take the cups and the dishes into the kitchen. Wipe, clean, scrub, remove and replace. I would like to change the sheets, but you are asleep. So, I slip under the cover next to you and try to find out how we, us, can bargain for more than 25 days. I message my sister, an oncology nurse in the States. Children – her cancers are young ones, but surely it is the same game. She tells me about alkaline food and coffee ground enemas. Some people believe, she is rather unsure. I will try the food, it makes sense, but the enemas might be a little too desperate, even for us. Are we desperate? I look at you. When you sleep, your breathing is even and deep. Better oxygen levels spell better chances. Alkaline food. Sensible food. Green and leafy. Kale, broccoli, spinach, and carrots. Tomatoes are good. Avocados and fish for fats. CBD oils for chemical balance. Making a list, I wonder how many people make lists like this at this moment, trying to gain days, hours, some even months. I have friends who have treated their tumours with hemp and they shrank. Your phone bleeps. Messages of support, calls for bravery and fight. How can you fight anything using just kale? Your fur-coated sister has left a pink quartz on the table. For healing she said. Green, leafy food and pink quartz, a new kind of science, but then it is better than Nothing. But it is not hope either. You stir, sit up, smile. We hold each other for a long time. 'Just us,' you say. And I feel peace for the first time in days. Peace, real peace. Just us.

Together we can beat anything, overcome anything, achieve anything. Together as one, we can walk this path, which is, despite the kale and the quartz, still likely to be a one-way street. I tell you about my findings, my sister's report, the coffee-ground enemas. You look slightly dismayed at the thought. But alkaline food is a good a programme as any. We have a plan. We will do something. You read your messages and I prepare sardines on brown rice. You eat, you are hungry. I love watching you eat. And after the gallons of water, we journey for most of the night, together, three legged, across the hall. There is a moment when I nod off. Not tired, just weary eyed. You return to your screen to watch grown men hitting each other, for no other reason than to feed their children and house their wives. I miss watching the news.

5

The Tree of Voices

A glorious morning. Cold, snow in the air. We are lying still, very still, as One. Not moving is respite. We are married 55 days, and, if we are lucky, have 24 left. The nine times table goes up at one side, whilst the other goes down. Directly opposing, counting up and down at the same time. We stare at the picture on the opposite wall. The tree, dead, painted by a friend, who gave it to me. A long time back, in the cottage. Do you remember the day in November, a few weeks after we met? We went to the cathedral where Holst is buried, and my friend exhibited his dismay to the public as art. I was supposed to go for some opening thing. But him understanding your presence would not have been possible. So, we went early, wandered around in the cold space, gothic walls, bits of glass and steel posturing as art or interpretation of faith amongst the solid, square stones. His paintings, you understood them. You stared for a long time, you touched and whispered. You understood. The voices he hears, the fear, the confusion – you understood. You understood his fight between medication and art. His wish to be pain free but scared of losing his paintings. We walked back to the car that day and spoke about your sister. Lovely sister, humble, quiet, loving, destroyed by your father and genetics. Hearing things, breaking herself, not wanting to break others. Lovely sister, whom I was yet to meet. So, we stare at the tree at the foot of our bed, reliving, tracing the lines with our eyes, willing the dead tree to live.

Scrambled egg, you try toast. Your coffee is milky now. There is pain, lots of pain, your face reflects the scrunches, emanating from just below your ribs. You eat the egg. I massage your skin around the swelling. Oil, Sarah made that oil for our wedding. A night we never had. I cannot place the smell, but you love it, and it is to become your smell from now on. I press a little too hard and you wince. I kiss you and your swollen skin. You draw me closer. We can overcome everything. We walk as one, think as one, survive as one. Will we give up as one? I want to, I need to be wherever you are. I need to keep you and the little one safe. No time any longer to linger. I have to meet your youngest from the station, she does not know where to go. And I do not trust the robot voice that could guide her. I take my pink fur from the hook. Look at you. I don't like looking back at you. I love looking forward and seeing you approach. No more of that. Never again will you walk towards me. I realised that last night, on our endless, relentless walks to the bathroom. We laughed. An old joke between us. Between us we make two good legs. Between us we can move forward, where each on their own would fail. I hesitate in the doorway, you wave your hand, pick up your phone. You never used to read messages before, maybe days later, reluctant, cursing under your breath. Always wondering what on earth people wanted you to do now. If you had the strength or the will to comply. Now you send messages. Keep them informed. Record videos, being upbeat. Looking like a fighter, strong, determined. The outside not matching your soul anymore. Your soul, brittle in my hands, flutters, denies, is looking for strength to hold on to. Do I have that? Hold on to me, please. And let's pray that I can stand. It is cold, snowing. It does not snow here, ever. The last time a few years ago. Not much, small white flurries. Insignificant. Landing on the pink fur. I call your youngest, we meet halfway. The robot voice has send her to me, to you, to us. We hug in the whispery flurry beside the green where we used to put concerts on every summer. So long ago. Lifetimes away. Before pandemics, before you, before us, before swollen livers and sunken eyes. Your youngest is of the half-empty persuasion. Recently, she has worked with the dead and the dying. Fancies herself as a nurse. We will talk about helping her study. For now, a little knowledge spells a dangerous road. We return to the flat. No longer a bubble, no longer at peace. She is big, loud, breaking, and brisk. You indulge, your love for her visible as much as your despair at her presence. We laugh, make jokes. I leave to work for a while. And shop. Shop for green leafy things and bottles of herbs, capsules of goodness. B12, cod-liver oil, green tea extract, and turmeric tea.

The snow does not settle. Not enough of it, not cold enough, or warm enough, I never know which. But certainly, too much salt in the air. I come back, with my bags clanging against my legs. Bringing swirls of cold air into the warmth of our rooms. You are asleep. Your youngest playing a game on her phone. We talk. We talk about her sister and the message she sent. How she did not want to upset you, how she thought she had been reasonable and fair. I assure her, again and again. I try to explain her sister's pain without telling your story. Not mine to share. What is mine to share? What can be said without betrayal? What is just mine? Not time, not space, not you, not our story even. Shared, invaded, taken over, belittled, taken into another world that I don't understand. You wake at the sound of the doorbell. Startled at first, but quickly finding your bearings. You smile at your sister. Gentle, disturbed, atoms of love floating amongst the dust. Speaking deliberately and slow, as if to trace words with her fingers, as if to make them real first. Kind eyes, soft skin. Her name means princess. Her companion, small, squad and Irish, is jolly with dark, sad eyes. Talk about allotments and potatoes, I think. His words are soft and pearly and hard to understand. I nod, smile, sit next to you on my pillows. Holding your hand. Peace. Outside, the insubstantial flurry continues, and I stare at the sky through the window. Clear blue with white dancing speckles. The hospital floor. Blue, speckled, clean. My feet flat next to each other. I shudder. A lifetime ago, maybe two. Before I had strangers as children and nephews and anger and tears clung to the air in our refuge. The Irish voice lulls me to sleep. It blurs and purrs, lovely, pleasant. Your sister is holding your other hand. Does she know that I know? Would she want me to know about the witchcraft? The Jamaican way of conjuring spirits, used by your father. A child, torn between her father's dark magic and her mother's church going. Abuse by a different name. Sending her into places nobody should go. Episodes they call them. Abyss of uncalled voices and pictures. Dark candles and Pentecostal singing; chant in an unholy duet. I look at her, small, beautiful lady, and can see the girl she once was – next to the boy you have been hiding from the world for so long. I shrug. Some things cannot be uttered, must not be said. You share them with me in the dark hours, have done for months. Suddenly, for no reason, I am back on our wedding day. You were tired then, not your usual spirit. Me questioning if it was a good plan. You held me tighter than ever. 'Yes, this is what I want, what I need.' I misunderstood your lack of excitement. You were sick then. I did not know. Did you know? Suspect? Did you know that you would make me a widow before I was a wife for a year? The nurse rings. She will see us on Wednesday. She has a kind voice, and you roll your eyes. You hate people with kind voices. We are in for a struggle. Her name is Aly, and you hate her already. You cannot bear pity and always mistake one for the other – kindness and pity are not the same. Compassion means suffering with you. Old Latin lessons I thought were forgotten flood back like the snowflakes and melt. The passions of Christ. The same word for love and desire and pain. So, I feel passion for us. No compassion with you, because we are One, the same pain, the same love, the same air. A difficult concept for others to see, to grasp. I felt with you, whatever you felt, from the beginning of sinking into your eyes. I saw the young one, right in the beginning. He began to peek around corners not much later than that. A quiet day, a good day. They all leave early. 'Just us', you sigh as you lean back into the pillows and hold my hand. We used to lay so close together. You can no longer lay on your side, and I have to be careful. Touch now can mean pain.

We turn our attention from the inside to the out, the wider, the news. I cannot take in the number of deaths, the hospital beds filled with skin that wants to survive. I cannot take in twitterings and orange men retreating to golf courses. But I startle at the translator of poems, who is rejected from weaving beauty and meaning into another language because she is of the wrong colour. How can words have a colour? How can poems be biased for or against anyone's race? Not sensitivity, but madness. You nod, slowly, deliberately. Your thoughts somewhere else. For a moment, a very brief, fleeting moment, I had forgotten. It was like it was in the cottage, or the first months building this bunker of love. I had forgotten about the Nothing, the growth in your belly, the time, the days, the remainder and the future that might never come. I come back with a start.

Back into the room with the tree at the end of our bed. Come back, realising, that it is harder to leave our passion and then to return. With every return it is harder, more painful, less gracious. You hold me, I hold you, for a very long time. In the darkness, I can just make out small, paper-like fragments of white.

6

The Ancients

Cold sun, bright blue sky. I should clean the windows. Should have done so a long time ago. Always finding a reason to wait. We used to have time, I used to have time and squandered it. The concept of time, artificial and crucial. Given to all of us and ticking away. I have a plan. We do not have time any longer, so I make a plan. To at least let you touch a little of the future we planned. For five minutes, for 15 minutes, once. Stonehenge. We will go. I can make it happen. If I can keep us alive until they re-open. I Google. It is possible. You can touch it. You can breathe in the ancients, the ones we have been exploring during the pandemic. We made drawings, references, speculated, read, ordered books. We spent days, weeks, months drawing up maps, looking for parallels between cultures and artifacts. You were open to universe visits, to gods misunderstood and lost on their travels. Me, more sceptical, less universe, more continental drift. We hunted the cradle, the beginning, the absolute 0 or 1. Made plans to travel. Where to begin? Petra, or Turkey or Africa? Maybe Syria, maybe Russia. All places open to us, to the future. Saving money, going cheap, touching stone to feel souls and knowledge long lost. We had time. But I can do small things. I pick up the phone. We can go to Stonehenge. With support, in the wheelchair if needed. You can touch it, the stone. You can find some wisdom. We both might need it, that wisdom long dead. The ancients died younger, or older. Did they know? Did they count down days as we do? We can go. We can take one of the busses, the purple ones I work from. We can go. With the help of some friends, who do not ask questions. I ask for Stonehenge and they will take us there. Two hours' drive, I think you can manage in the bus, with me holding your hand. You are feeling strong, this is a good day. I can fetch your youngest from Arundel station. I can leave you for the duration. For the time that it takes to fetch her and fly back. I am not telling you about my plan. It is my plan for Us. Organised, dates to be arranged and confirmed, but soon. We do not have the time to wait for days. We are married 56 days. Nearly 60, that is an achievement. Can we make 60? There is no reason not to presume so. You look better. I make smoothies. The parcels and boxes and packets have started to come to the door. Your work has sent a hamper of cheese, tea, and crackers, all organic, because organic is good. You want to read, but your eyes cannot focus. Your mind is not willing to stare at letters and make sense out of them. Another parcel sent by your eldest, coconut water, heavy. Tomorrow there will be the nurse. I can ask questions, find out. There are so many things I don't know.

I am not trained, have no experience; I am, after all, new. But I can ask and listen and learn. Your youngest daughter, with her half-empty glass, sits next to me now, telling me how bad things are. What could happen. My eyes sting. No need to cry. I will learn. I can learn. The nurse can tell me what I need to know. I have learned about apricot kernels. Nature's chemo apparently. Not too many though, that would be poison. I ordered the kernels; they will arrive tomorrow. I am learning about CBD oil, properties of tomatoes. Whenever you sleep, I learn. Diagrams, notes, asking questions, finding out. I can learn to keep things static, not to let them get worse. Like when getting attacked at work – make safe, don't try to defend at first – make safe. Things are bad, we know this. But how bad, nobody can tell. And if we can arrest things at this stage, maybe, just maybe, we can make it past 28 days.

You said Cheltenham was a goal. The first of March is a goal. We have many, small ones to reach. We can, with green, leafy veg, apricot kernels, and love. We can. I can take you in a purple bus to Stonehenge. A small place, compared with Petra, but small things matter, too. We arrive home. And again, the visits begin. Your daughter, with her daughters. I smile. More complications. Who is blood and who counts? They all count to you. I know that, you know that. They surely know that. The sisters, who are also cousins. Years of hurt, misunderstanding, resentment. And you in the middle, extracting yourself to the bookies or Bristol or Liverpool.

Three years after your eldest was born, you took up with another. Already two children. Small, ready to have you as their father. You were ready to be a father to them. As far as you ever could be a father, as far as you understood being a man. Still young. Still so full of future that consequences did not enter your mind. The girl you took up with and stayed for long after, was, after all, the sister of your eldest child's mother. You always went with the familiar, still do. You think there is less chance to get hurt. You stayed or you went, for ease. Scared of too many new things. Do you remember when we first went to the Chinese to pick up some food? Small village, green, sleepy, empty on that Sunday night. You were weary, kept looking around you, checking for enemies in the dark. I laughed. You wanted to wait in the car. Your saunter more quiet, less forward. Yes, familiar is important to you. You stared at the trees in the carpark, dressed in their new knitted blankets. Knitted by children during their school hours, to keep the trees warm. You could not penetrate the unfamiliar, the new, the strange, and lifted the bottle again and again. Jack Daniels that day. Most days. Sometimes rum, mostly brown, amber, and oily, a strong smell that seared my nostrils. You let the liquid dissolve in your mouth, before it entered your throat, slowly. A good day. I could tell by the way of your drinking. There was savouring, melting some days, and gulping, hardly swallowing on others. I knew better than you. Observing, analysing, reading. Whenever I drank your eyes into mine, you knew I was reading. Then, not transmitting, that came much later, when you had learned to read me. I was reading your story and I still do. Only now I know more. I transmit more. I write more onto the back of your eyes. Our room, full of smoke, I open the window. You, holding court. The granddaughters next to your shoulders. You drawing tattoos for their arms or their ankles. They will ask the man with the needle to paint your drawings onto their skin. Their big, hooped earrings glinting in the fading light, like their mother's before. Today is a good day. You are happy, I can see. You have me take photos. On everyone's phone. I hold five phones in my hand, including yours, and take the same picture, time and again. There are now at least 30 versions of you, in the same pose. In our bed. Sitting up, looking proud. And suddenly I realise, that your face has grown smaller somehow. Looking at the pictures, you seem to have shrunk. A little, imperceptible, not noticeable in the half light of the room. But yes. You are smaller.

They leave, you are smiling at me, laying back in the pillows. I fluff the blanket, just for something to do. You hold my arm for a moment, looking at me, scanning, reading. I close my eyes. There are things you don't need to see. But you see them, you know, you feel what I feel. My sudden wish to shrink with you, so that we are still the same in proportion. I want to tell you about the purple bus and Stonehenge, the wheelchair, the friends who will guide us and hold us, so that you can touch the stone. But I say nothing. Something does not seem right. You ask me for rice with sardines and I make my way into the kitchen. You eat, I am happy. Tomorrow there will be the nurse and she will teach me how to be, what to do. She will tell me about all of the things that are mysterious to me now. And I do hope my glass stays half full. You kiss me, gentle as always. I hold your face in my hands. Your cataract eyes are bluer than ever, hiding the brown underneath.

7

A New Soldier

57 days ago, I became a wife, your wife. You a husband, my husband. I never wanted to be anyone's anything. Possessiveness is grammatical. You have a name, your name, I have mine. Husbandry means farming, growing, looking after and care. Care is what we have for each other, and love and acceptance. Care for you is care for me. Not separate. Your bones are mine and my skin is yours. Holding you is keeping me in one piece. Us, we, one. You never had a wife before. You are proud still, saying it every morning. 'Good morning, my wife.' And I smile. You can no longer turn to kiss me; I have to lean up and over you. But your hand can still lay on my neck, warm and comforting. I need comfort, warmth, I need you. You are not hungry today; swallowing is a chore. Your breathing, laboured and short, has now changed your voice. You whisper, speak slower. Losing confidence in your words. Often you don't remember the phrases. I finish your sentences. You are grateful for my little intrusions. You ask me, often, what something means. My biggest fear? Before this started, before Nothing lived in your belly, my biggest fear was your brain. When you suspected the lungs, I found out all I could. And it likes to go from the lungs to the brain. You had headaches, terrible headaches. I did not tell you what I feared. Your beautiful brain, born like a phoenix, coming to life. Taking everything in, beginning to see the small things, beginning to open like amaryllis in spring. I used to have some at the cottage, and you marvelled at the red streaks running delicately through white petals on

35

stubbornly upright stems.

A drink, you will take a drink. Not coffee, too bitter today. I fill the blender with milk, cream, avocado, and honey. Green, creamy fluid. You drink. You nod, I feel happy. You drink, swallow, care seeping into your body. My care, our care. Today, the nurse will tell us what we can do. Practical, logical, from experience and training. She will know what I should do to make you better. Better is an illusion, but I can make you stronger, I hope. She will come in the morning, she said. I have to leave you at lunchtime. Work, like swallowing, has become an unbearable chore. I fetch your youngest from the station whilst you are checking your messages. Outpouring of love. Collective and personal wishes for health and strength. You want your youngest to assist me, to help me whenever she can. But she is brittle, fragile, any small thing could hurt her, because the big ones already have. You are beginning to realise that. Maybe you see her for the first time in all her glorious colours. Like you, a clown, an entertainer with darkness hidden inside her. Psychotic moments.

Bad, dark moments. We will talk about how much she can take. She will sit with you whilst I wander the wilderness of other people's minds. There is snow in the air. Pictures from the other side of the Downs show blankets of whiteness. I like snow. Everything new, everything silent, echoing, the sky lower somehow. Nothing bad can happen in snow. A long time ago, under a skylight, in a distant country that was my home, I lay in my bed, with my mouth wide open, trying to drink in the clean, crisp newness it brings. You, more pragmatic, smile at my excited eyes, scanning the window for the first sign, coiled, ready to pounce into the garden. I leave, driving slowly. Leaving you with your youngest. The nurse is late, and I am going to miss her. How can I learn if I cannot ask questions? I sigh. I call on arrival, your youngest says you are fine. I am not to worry. I am not worried, but I am not there, and I miss you. I do not have time not to spend with you. I cannot lose any more seconds of Us. On the other side of the Downs, the snow is more snowlike. In places it settles. I stare at the sleeves of pink fur. In a village shop I find Weetabix in small bottles. Because I cannot decide and the constants of taste are shifting, I buy every flavour for you. I drive home, much faster, flakes hitting the windscreen and melt into small lakes of ice-white paint splashes, disappearing as rivers of clear water.

In the beginning, in the very beginning, the first winter, you scraped the ice from the car in the mornings. With Us I learned to wake up at a time when I used to come home. You never had breakfast, just a swig from yesterday's bottle. I shuddered watching you, but it never felt strange. It was you; what you did. And I said that it was between you and your liver. I was sure that you, one day, would stop. Medication no longer needed, wounds healing from inside out, no longer needing their cover. The core of your wounds, the boy, safe, cradled in the crook of my arm. Blanketed and soft, warm and at home. Pain oozing away with memories of a house without beds, black candles, dead children, and you clinging onto a mother who had already gone to live with the voices that would take her away. You are hazy about dates, backstories, and history. There is a shortage of facts. Your mother, from an important family, half Indian, already unmarried mother to three, left Jamaica for England in '58 with you in her belly, bringing only one daughter with her. Your mother, small, with straight long Indian hair, on a journey into the cold, the unknown, was to bear at least nine more children. For the man she followed, who tortured, controlled, and finally broke all of you.

On my return, your eyes are bright, excited, you are happy. You gave the nurse a hard time, as we knew you would. Mischief: you like mischief nearly as much as you dislike people with soft voices. I kiss you. 'What did she say?' Nothing much, she prodded and poked, asked questions, took notes. She has been ordering medicine, more medicine, and more morphine that you just will not take. 'Know the enemy', biblical mantra. We talk about pain, steroids, and morphine. Why suffer if you don't have to? Why embrace pain if you could embrace time. Chose Weetabix over whiskey, love over Nothing. Chose. Your youngest talks about bedsores and funeral plans. I stare at her. Blank. I know nothing about one or the other. Bedsores are graded, I learn. Later I am to find out that her grading was wrong, but by then it will not matter anymore. Today is the sixth day after that day, when our world became a flurry of lesions, secondaries, primaries, morphine, Nothing, mad growing cells, strange children and nephews, emotions that were not ours, but rooted in you. I stare at you. You, wide eyed, handing over to me all thoughts of dressings, bedsores, nutrition and apricot kernels, chuckle softly into your nest of pillows. 'Not yet,' you say, 'not yet. Try not to worry, no cause for concern.' And I know that you're lying, and you know that you are lying, but between us this is the new truth. Accepted, filed away to cloak us.

Six days since we found that time is a commodity that can run out, that cannot be replaced. I take your youngest back to the station. The snow is no longer falling on this side of the Downs, whilst Scotland and Croydon and Crawley are covered in white. Back in our shelter, our safe space, cleansed now of all the unsettled and unsettling, we curl up, holding each other, exhausted, hungry for life, but unable to eat. And you point at the bottle. Liquid morphine, glistening in the light of your lamp. The lamp that does not need buttons, or switches, just touch. On and off light, whenever I dust or you move, unintentional, uninvited flickering between moments of touch. Our hands merge, hard, strong. We stare at the tree at the end of the bed because the ceiling is too far out of reach. You stared at that ceiling for weeks before. 'Yes,' you say, 'why not.' A teaspoon, a small dose. The first sign of surrender. Maybe we are not as strong as we thought. Or we just accepted a new soldier into our army, to join turmeric, CBD oil, and green vegetables. Maybe combining the steroids with the morphine can form another torpedo to buy us some time. I open the bottle. Despair and gladness flowing onto the spoon. Sticky. You open your mouth. Thinking about it, you never once, not once, opened that bottle yourself.

8

Morphine and Wine

We are still here. Stronger. Better. You slept. No pain during the night. Your face less drawn, less pale. Your eyes brighter. I stroke your chin, the back of your ears. You have beautiful ears. You ask for scrambled eggs. In the kitchen, I mix small pieces of beacon into the egg, herbs, beetroot, and butter. The cat, next to me, hopes for leftovers. No family today. Just people, I draw my jumper, the Big Snuggly, around my shoulders. Shiver in the icy morning light. Air flooding in, cold air, through the backdoor, open for the cat to escape. Seven days since the hospital. One week, still singular, so nothing to worry about. We have a new morning routine. Steps on our path into battle. Me, who hates routines nearly as much as platitudes, suddenly holding on to rituals as if they can save us. Three pills and some drops. After the egg. B12, Omega 2 and green tea extracted into white pellets. You swallow. Life, care, warmth, hopefully days. You are excited about your visit today. Three girls from your work. I am surprised. They are not from the warehouse; they are from upstairs. Seven days less; 58 days your wife. Do you count? I play with my ring, meandering back. Another day in winter, before Christmas in the cottage. I wanted to visit a friend. Arundel, Tarrant Street. His studio open for Christmas, like every year for the season. You, half drunk at ten in the morning, stood in the doorway. Held me for a brief moment. Inhaled at the back of my neck, 'I love your smell, I need your smell.' My glasses cluttered onto the floor, and I held you, held us. My friend was not there,

40

exhibitions elsewhere, but his wife was. Near to the fire, pointed at stollen and wine. You had the wine. I did not know her, just wandered through rooms full of paintings and heavy air. I stood very close and felt nothing. Beauty at distance does not always spell beauty in person. I wanted to see the strokes of the brush that I so loved as small pictures on screens. I wanted to learn, to understand. You followed, laughed at my trying. We stood in the middle of the white room, in a puddle of sunlight, watery winter air, and held each other, far enough from the canvass to be able to see. The rivers, the lakes, the meadows, the sunrise. I shook my head, disappointed. Something so beautiful from a distance, so ordinary and flat up close. We returned to the fire, and you filled your glass, less urgent, more assured. Making conversation with the woman whose rooms we invaded in the interest of art. She noticed my accent. Said I sound like her mother. She came from a place a few streets away from my school. Came here as a child, but still steeped in foreign traditions, habits, familiar to me. We sat, three strangers, in front of a fire, you drinking wine, Willow and I comparing recipes for stollen and jam. The world, endless pearl necklace of coincidences and fate, was ours to explore, to fill as we wished. We had time to return next Christmas and bring wine of our own. Willow embraced us and we returned to the cold, cobbled street where, in the summers, I sit and chalk on the stones.

The present is just a bad dream, we have had all the good ones. I will wake soon, and we will make plans. For the weekend, the summer and springs, there will be endless springs. The cat jumps on the visitor's bags. Lovely young ladies. They brought food and wine. I am not sure about the wine, but what harm can it do now? You ask for more morphine as if for a gift. I sit next to you, on my pillow. Laughter, smiles, stories. Humanity at its best. Sparkling affection. Compassion and warmth. Care. They care. Like we care for each other. They care for you, for us. My eyes sting, but only a little. Yours sparkle, happy, surprised at this care, surprised how you touched them over the years. I hold your hand, listen, enchanted. Another facet of your prism revealed. Light air, true laughter, willing us on to live. There is care, so much attention. Steroids, it is time for your afternoon steroids. Your skin will grow thinner, more brittle with time. I will use my skin to keep your bones warm. As they prepare to leave, a blond girl with sincere hands takes me aside. I am not to worry; they will keep you in work. They will do anything in their power to keep our journey untroubled from what is outside. They will protect us from wolves. All of them will. They love you. Without condition, without expectation. They shine in our rooms like twinkles of hope and out in the garden I cry a couple of tears. For what you gave them, the bonds lost, the love, the years you will miss. And even a little for the delivery drivers who made you late for your train.

You are not hungry, but I have made soup. Feeling guilty for not feeding your visitors, I made a large pot. You eat. I can see the warm fluid calming your throat. We talk. Plans. Retrospective. Can we make plans backwards? Can we shrink them until they fit into this? We talk about your work, the people around you. The people you choose. The ones you did not think would notice you. Calling yourself the biggest underachiever for too many years. Having failed at so much, or so you believe. Small things count. You must see that. And I know you have learned, over the months, to look freshly at things. Small things matter, the moon at our window. We only ever see one side, the other one always hidden. You always looked at one side of you. Now, we are Us, you can see the whole sphere. You suddenly, with a jolt, understand what you mean to others. The little things, the words, the gestures, the not going home when you should. The cigarette breaks, the jokes, and the wisdom. They stay in their minds when the storms have passed, dramas avoided and everyone, bar you, has gone home.

There never was need for your bravado, the big man, the hiding.

The little things that form the prism, that is you – they matter. They have always mattered, only you did not know. You thought what mattered was what others already had. A life, a home, children around scrubbed pine tables. Nobel prizes and cars that were not nicked. We are married for 58 days. More morphine, the pain rips through you. Earthquakes, tsunamis, fault lines of pain. I hold you; you grip my hand. Hard, harder, make the pain seep into me. I can take it. I can take pain but feeling yours is unbearable. Hand over the pain, breathe. The morphine will help. Breathe it away. It will pass. Your body straining and your eyes rolling. You scream, I scream inside. I understand, this is not Nothing. These are the cells they can do nothing about. They grow like an embryo in the wrong place and tear you apart. Are they your cells? Have you made them? Creator of pain. After what might have been hours, seconds, days, you feel soft, warm, home again. The pain has subsided. I know that we will not be sleeping. You want to watch the enemy. You want to know when he is coming and what he is doing. Anticipate, pre-empt. Wounded, but not beaten, not yet. Seven days ago, I had a monitor, with little red letters and bleeping and lilac paper walls. Now, I have nothing to gauge your internal struggle. Your head on my shoulder. Exhausted. I make coffee, just for me. Your cup remains empty. Water, more water. Morphine makes you thirsty. Dehydration spells repeated collapse. A good day, a very good day. Happy, a few hours ago, we were happy. Now, we are just raw humanity; wounded beings clinging onto each other. The trips to the bathroom begin. More water, more faltering steps. More morphine. How is this possible? Two days ago you refused and now it has become part of you. Like the wine and the whiskey, and the rum and the brandy. No lucky dip for us. Tonight, we are not lucky. Tomorrow we might. Tomorrow we might find the solution, the right dose in time. I did not know, there is no ceiling on morphine. You can take as much as you like. You can take more morphine than wine. You rest and I find out about background doses and acute pain. The balance. You always said one needs balance. And you were right. We just have to find it; and find it soon.

9

Blood

59 days of being your wife. I still have not changed my name. There has not been time yet. 59 days since Mick and your youngest bore witness in a corridor in Crawley. Wearing masks, everyone distanced, apart from us. Beautiful, simple day. Me feeling overdressed for the occasion. You could not do up the bottom of your suit trousers. You did not swig that morning, had not done in some time. Healing, after all this time. Healing from the inside out. There was nothing to swig in the house. We set off in the morning, early, to avoid traffic. Collected your youngest. After, we had some spare time and searched for a coffee. Happy, so happy, and glad. We found coffee and sat. Your youngest and us. She was not sad when she told us, but told us nevertheless. The man she was hoping to marry had cheated on her – recently. Your face became stony, happiness evaporated like air from a volcano. You never liked him before, but now you were ready to kill. I locked onto her face; her eyes averted from mine. Why now? Why tell us now? Why not tomorrow, or yesterday or whenever? Why now? When we were happy and skipping into a new, brighter future and were going to meet him for lunch. Your breath, sharp, angry, and sad, flew across the table, unsettled the coffee. She smiled. You needed a drink. Your eyes pleading with mine, to go back, five minutes, ten minutes – go back and make things unsaid. We had lunch, the four of us, with unspoken truths between us, hanging in the air, poisoning steaks and ice cream. Three whiskeys later, we drove home. Some photos taken that I have yet to see. We went to the beach,

sat on the stones, not speaking, each in thought of the other. Broken and whole at the same time. You held me, tighter than ever. Buried your nose in the nape of my neck. My hair irritating your nose. And we went hom after the beach and cried, because we were happy and starting again. With our future marred by the past. But a future, nevertheless. You said it was time. We should leave, soon. A friend, my best friend, trying to find work for me, back in my country. We looked at places to live and calmed.

Today is the first day, when weeks are plural for us. After seven days, we have only plurals of week. Closer and closer to Nothing. We lie still for a long time, before the caregiving pills and the shakes full of green and honey. Eight days since diagnosis. Eight days since the chairs started to break. You look stronger today. The cat has taken residency at your feet. You start to record video clips and send them in groups, waiting for replies. Eager, excited, words – willing you on. Dry sense of humour that is not humour at all. You soak up, drink in the new love. Their warmth sustains us. Friends, you thought you never had friends. And you learn, by the hour, how important you are.

Two faces has the moon, one is hiding. I need to potter, straighten, clean. I feel guilty for being noisy and unsettling your nest. You draw me closer. 'I like it. Be busy. It reminds me of normal.' And so I do, be busy, inconsequentially dusting, mopping, moving. For something to do, for you to listen to noises. Normal. We are ok, for now.

You are on a call. I go to the shops. Cigarettes and lucky dips, cat food and milk. Visitors today. Liberty family, you cannot remember who. They love you; you love them and so I love them too. Cheese, they bring cheese and wine. Expensive wine, chosen by the directors. I am grateful. Not for the wine – the gesture. The thought. The care. Husbandry, I think, at its best and I miss my sheep. I say little, busy myself, but can hear the happy tone in your voice. Grateful, happy – I am grateful for what they give you. It lessens the pain, makes things shinier and easier. The flat glows. You glow. Today, a little morphine goes a long way. Your daughter, the one whose place in the order of age I cannot gauge, rings. She is not your eldest, but the same age. Not the same skin, but your child nevertheless. She cries. The eldest has given her fear. That she might be excluded, along with her brother, from what is to come – after. I puzzle about the After. When? What After? Funerals are for those to be buried. Not you, not us, not yet, not for a long time. Why excluded? They are your children. 'Not blood,' she says, 'not blood.' Your eldest has talked about blood, and fathers that require the pronoun 'my'. Possession again, pressed into language. How can a person belong in this way, to any other person? Blood rebuilds over time, replenishes, renews, not the same blood as it was yesterday. The sisters, cousins, inextricably linked by time and resentment, neglect and despair. Their mothers, sisters, orbiting around you and each other. Their children, vessels of hate. I freeze, nothing to draw on. Trying to make it better. I hold her over the phone with my words. She matters, they matter, but really – you matter most. You cannot make good on mistakes made by the boy. Not now, not ever. Not enough time in eternity to go back and undo. I return to the room. Your face still glowing and happy, talking, joking, relaxed. No pain. I sit next to you and stroke your neck. Your beautiful neck. And I startle. Your skin is too loose. It has never been loose. Like a turtle or a tortoise, but softer. New folds where missing flesh was. I scan your face, what I can see of your body. Nothing has changed. You kiss me, 'my queen, my rock', and I know I will not tell you about the fears of your daughters and sons. I will protect them when the time comes. You don't touch the cheese and only a little of wine. Too strong in their taste for your tortoise-skinned throat. Eight days after that day, you are growing and moulding into your new role. The Don, the wise one. Being paid homage to. Passives are treacherous things. Paying homage is easy, accepting it is not.

After the visit, we curl up in the warm afternoon light. 'Just us,' you say, 'just us'. You smile and we draw closer, well I draw closer to you. More morphine. The doorbell. The son with your name. He sits on a chair, more comfortable than he has been before. You talk, we talk. I give you space. You ask him to look after me, when all this is over. Some grand scheme, possibly as smart as your lucky dips. I don't know, I go to the other room and busy myself. When I return, we talk about his children, his future, his life. He is like you, and so different. You tell him that he wants to hand me over to him, for protection. My head hurts. How can anyone hand anyone over? I don't need protection, not now, not ever. He accepts, nevertheless. You, who thinks him weak and me strong wants him to be my protector. From what? From whom? And here it is again – the After. The weeks. The days. How many are left? Do you know? I try to read the space behind your eyes. After he leaves, we talk. Why him? And there it is. 'My eldest blood son.' I look at you for a long time. Your gaze does not waiver. I sit up next to you. You read my thoughts, imperceptibly shaking your head. Your thinking that of your father, destroyer of life and everything good. In the end, we cling to what is familiar, thoughts of our fathers. Their sins perpetuated in us. We return to what we did not want to be. You roll a cigarette, inhale. Red tip in the faltering light. You chose who you are. Like in that dream you had a few months ago. We curl into each other again. Too short the time until we begin our endless dance between the pillows and the bathroom again.

10

129 Bottles

We are still here. 60 days married and day nine of our lifetime together, awaiting the end of the sentence. I send messages – we are still here. Celebrating the day. During the night, at four in the morning, still talking, you suddenly saw what you had said. You shuddered, shivered, shrugged, and cried. Your blood is going to hurt you. Others will not. Your Liberty family is not blood. I am not blood. And yet we are one. But words spoken and thought cannot climb back into the tomb of your tongue. You had it said to you, many times. And when he died, your father left messages all over the house. Proof, so he thought, of a slight, of untruth and you not being his blood. Written in black ink all over the house, where you nursed your mother. Your prison for three long years. Your prison of tea, your mother's dreams, strange memories from a time before you, forgetting the hurt and staring out of the window. Why are cups of tea lovely and coffee just strong? We are tired, exhausted, empty of thought. But full of feeling, for each other, for Us, for the tree at the end of our bed. No fear yet, that will come later. 'Nescafe,' you say, sleepy. Your tastebuds have changed. You return to old preferences. Sweet things and cheese, avocado and olive oil, sardines on rice, spices and Aloe-Vera.

We are expecting your eldest. I can go and get coffee and cat food and flowers. For a short while, I have to leave our den, our cloche of love. But I will be back, I promise, as quick as I can. Bring in provisions, for you and the cat. And tissue for all of those tears, shed by others, far too early and all over your chest. I am not ready for tears yet. Maybe I never will be. I hold you. Your eyes tired. 'Go,' you say, 'just go. And come back.' So, I go, leaving your eldest in the kitchen, making herself some peppermint tea. Leaving her with my most precious, with what has become me, my life, my future. Leaving you with her past. The lights outside are too bright, too noisy for the back of my eyes. Floating amongst other's reality. No avocados. But fruit. Blackberries, blueberries, strawberries, oranges, and kiwi. Water, lots of water. I find fast hydrating water, protein enriched. I am learning, I have to learn fast. Learn things I never thought would be of any importance at all. Flowers, your mother used to buy flowers. Like me, she craved beauty. I return, your eldest next to you. In my bed, on my pillow, next to you. Looking at me, glinting and hinting. I smile. A child. A lost child abused and discarded. Her mother pimping her out. Taking her places to go to the shops and not returning for days. Leaving her on yours and her sister's doorstep fourteen years later. Unmanageable. I can hear from the kitchen an unknown voice. And yet I know. I just know, my body stiffens, bile in my throat. I turn to the doorway. And there she is, holding her phone to your face. Her mother. She is coming. Next Sunday. I shake. Anger, betrayal. But I smile. What can I say? What is my place? Where is my sanctuary, my truth? Coffee, more coffee. Unspeakably tired and weary, I lean against the kitchen door. Your eldest approaching, smiling. I turn away. You frown, scanning my face. I am hiding, behind the cup, steaming. Hiding in the steam, so that you cannot see my pain. Betrayal, of you, of me, of words spoken to safeguard Us. I read your new turtleneck skin. More morphine, more steroids. Pain begins to wash over us. Your pain in my bones. When your eldest leaves, I ring the number. Nurses, I need help. I don't understand. Don't know enough. They will come on Monday.

We are clinging onto each other until the pain subsides, washed away by sticky liquid on teaspoons. Painkillers do not deal with the source of the pain; they numb the nerves that tell us about it. They blunt nerve endings and receptors, and we don't know that we are in pain anymore. You relax back into my arms. I hold you. And suddenly, you look at me and ask for your mum. You want your mother. I kiss you, all over your beautiful face and tell you she is no longer able to hold you, in truth, she never really was. But you are held, loved, watched over and cared for. You are a part of a bigger self, important and beautiful and at home. You have a home, a cat, and soft pillows. You said, in the cottage, 'there is nothing bad here'. We settle, more coffee and I read you a chapter of 'Once'. Miss Essex upstairs is having a party. She cannot hold her drink and in a couple of hours there will be door slamming and crying. We eat Jaffa cakes. I still do not like them, but if I eat, you will. You talk about your eldest and her mother, the aunt to the others, by blood either way. You talk of revenge and lessons to be taught. I don't believe you but bite my tongue. I have told you; it never matters what a person does. Their reasons matter. I have always explored reasons, grappled for understanding, so that I can create order. I need to understand, to make sense of it all and accept it for what it might be. 'I need to teach her, that she is not the only important one. I am teaching her something that she will need in her life.' I question your methods. 'Mischief,' you say, 'I can still cause mischief.' And I believe that you hold this as true.

There was a night in the winter of 2019. You worked late, you needed to finish 129 bottles, picking, labelling, and boxing. I rang. Trains would not wait for you to finish a task. They have their own agenda, their own track, their own time. You forgot and missed the last one. But you picked, labelled, and boxed 129 bottles, ready to go to a cruise ship for rich people to sample. You walked all night. From station to station, trying to find somewhere that could move you closer to home. We were on the phone, you sent pictures all night. The bottle of amber emptying into your throat, keeping you warm. And you walked and walked and bought a burger for someone who sat outside one of the stations. You talked to him for a while, talking to me at the same time.

At six in the morning, I collected you at last from the station in the village. You were tired and dirty and a bit more than drunk. You fell into the car, nestled your nose on my shoulder. Staggering into the cottage, you sighed 'home'. And I knew that you wanted to be here, with me, with us, with the cat. You needed to be here and not coming home had no meaning other than what it was. You had a task. It needed completing. Nothing bad here or there. You knew I would be waiting for you, in the warm cottage, with the cat and the books and our love. It is easy to love us. The one with so many sides. The one universe made from so many facets, that it shone in the windows and our eyes. And now we are here, and nothing has changed. Only the pain and the Nothing and the time we have left. And we love us. I hold you until you finally sleep. Soft snoring, deep breaths. We are still here.

11

Dancers

We sleep well, a good night. No dreams, no pain, no endless bathroom journeys. You record a video for the world. I make coffee, feed the cat. We have travelled through nine days. I am not thinking of counting the future. Today is a good day. You look bright and strong. Fighting talk. My queen and I have a plan. We will beat this. We will survive. A little more hesitant, I want to believe you. Looking at you, I have no reason to doubt. Maybe we can. Maybe we will, after all, travel to Egypt and Syria and Stonehenge. You, on your way to the bathroom, stumble. Fear, suddenly there is fear in your cheeks. It leaks from you like the pearls of rainwater on the windows. I need to wash the windows and clean the fridge. Streaks of fear down your forehead, collecting in the hollows of your collarbone. Reminiscence of the collapse in the corridor, between the vending machine and the pharmacy.

We knew, before, that an appointment so soon, a face-to-face meeting, would not spell good news. But we were prepared, in our heads, we were ready, we thought. We walked together on the shiny corridor floor. I was not yet accomplished in supporting your weight. I held your arm, you held mine. And suddenly, you, limp and breathless, leant into me and the wall. I held you, unsure, lost, screaming inside for help. A man, maybe a porter, rounded the corner, direction east wing. He stopped, looked at me and at you, at us. He asked if you always moved like that, fell like that. I stared, unable to answer, shaking my head. He took you from me, stronger arms, younger arms. He sent me to reception, to call for help. I ran, noisy footsteps echoing. Reception was slow. My eyes pleading, stinging, breath fast, confused and all I could feel was you. The man found me, running towards me. 'He needs you', running back, I could hear you screaming. People, at least 10, around you in a tight group of support you rejected. You wanted your wife, me. The first time ever, since I met you, maybe ever in your life, you needed someone. Me, your wife of 51 days. You heard me, tried to turn around. They held you, the crash team. I held your shoulders, kissed your face, tears, yours or mine I could not tell. Frightened, both of us. Fears fusing together in thought. You calmed a little. The crash team breathed, all ten of them, as with one lung. They breathed and you allowed them to lift you onto the bed. Separate corridors, separate journeys, one thought, one life in the balance – ours. The man from the corridor helped me to find you. Restrictions waved out of the way. I was grateful but could not remember my phone number when asked for the record. I could remember your date of birth, but not much else. I knew it began with a seven, but nothing beyond.

The receptionist had sad eyes, resting on me, telling me it did not matter. Maybe she was right, but I needed to remember. Some numbers, gone, important numbers, just gone. And then someone led me to the lilac curtain room. I look at you, as I pull the cover back over you. Your skin is grey. How can I do the right things if in a panic I cannot remember 10 numbers? How will I know what to do? How will you guide me? Your eldest is back. It is the weekend. Like all weekends from now on. I want to love her, want to help her through whatever this is. She wants her mother to find closure. Herself – redemption. I am not sure what you want. I wait. I will see. Clarity is important. No decisions made in haste are ever good ones. Reason must be the base of all things. More visitors, your eldest plays hostess. Confused when they don't address her. Liberty people, people with love and compassion for us. Extending good will to me because you are important to them. Holding me in their minds because I hold you in my heart. Coffee, endless coffee and tea. The cat at your feet revels in skin, caressing his fur. He has not moved since this morning. No need, love comes to him. You hold my hand. We can make it. We have made nine days so far. Nothing really bad happened. We have morphine and steroids and vitamin B. Now you ask me to help you before you attempt the arduous journey to the bathroom. We found a new way of walking. Not next to each other, but touching foreheads, me backwards, you following. More stable and time to rest and kiss on the way. We look like dancers. Our hands and fingers entwined. Slowly, but with purpose, we make our way round two corners. I am glad that we have lost the cottage. The cottage had steep, narrow stairs to the bathroom. Small rooms, a narrow boat filled with pictures and books, obstacles at every turn. We would not have survived in the cottage. It broke my heart when we had to leave. We were happy in the cottage. But your arrival changed things. Changed everything, although I did not realise that in the beginning. You took my attention away. You dominated my time and my thoughts. Our will to build a future was directly opposed to my past. The cottage was mine; this place is ours. And it is flat and roomy, and dancers can manage the corners without stabbing their toes.

I wait in the bathroom, stroking your neck. Sweat collecting under your brows. A long journey there and a long journey back. But we make it, you straighten your shoulders. 'Nothing to see peeps. I am fine.' The girls from HR take their leave. They promise to come again. They have parties to go to and friends to see. Your eldest will stay. I am tired and I know you are too. But she calls her children. You come alive. Grandchildren. They make you happy. No guilt, no resentment, no old wounds. They are new and fresh and young; they love you and you love them. No baggage to pull your shoulders back into the quagmire of past misdemeanours that you would rather forget.

12

Protein

You are awake all through the night. I sleep fitfully, fearing you might attempt to walk on your own. Proud man, strong man, unpredictable in your pride. I stroke your collarbone gently; it seems more sunken than yesterday. Deeper, softer, bonier. You kiss my hair and my eyes. 'Good morning, wife.' I smile, you smile, we are content. A wife of 62 days. Learning to be a nurse. Learning to hold Us, alone, without input from you. 'You are in charge, my queen.' I laugh. I never wanted to be in charge of anything. I am not good at giving directions. Guidance, yes, but directions are not my strong point at all. I have many talents, but managerially, I am a lost cause. I draw diagrams on your belly, trying to trace where the Nothing lives. Your hand on my back, my head on your chest, we are breathing as one. You reject coffee but will have tea. Warm, I believe warm fluid is good. In the kitchen, chopping, measuring, and blending, I feel my knees buckle. I sit on the floor, in front of the sink, where you cannot see me. The dishwasher whirls, familiar, but now overused sound. We used to fill it by Friday. Once a week was enough for the two of us. Now, it is working its hardest, cleaning cups, plates, whatever the visitors leave.

Composure, I need composure. We have managed 10 days, nearly two weeks. Two weeks is our lowest, smallest, and most frightening goal. Morphine and vitamins. Your language has changed. Your sentences shorter ... 'I want,' is your new favourite phrase. Your hand rests on my shoulder, there is something new in your eyes. I cannot place it – yet. On our way to the bathroom, strange tango invented for us, you stop, catch your breath and stare at the scales. You want to know how much of you has been lost. How much of you is already gone. I am reluctant. Sometimes not knowing is easier. Illusions can be a safe space. Ten days ago, we wanted to know, we thought that knowing was power. Now I feel that illusions have more power than truth. Illusions are months, years even. Knowing reduces us to days and weeks. The scales are not working, needing new batteries, I breathe a sigh of relief. I promise to buy some tomorrow, unsure if I should not forget. Tired, I am unspeakably tired. Your eldest, smelling of coconut oil and fresh shower, looks polished and pretty and young. She will leave around lunchtime. We talk, the three of us, around our bed. All I can see are the footprints, the crumbs, spillages, ash on the floor. We talk about her son, a spectrum boy with numbers as his best friends. She seems interested in what I have to say. Everything works if we find the right base. Not talking about the roots, the core, the pain is better, easier. We pass the morning, and she leaves, back to her life, feeling the dutiful daughter. I make some food; you try to eat. We are both tired, so very tired. We talk for a short while about 'after'. You don't want me to come with you. I promise to do my best. Best endeavours as always. You say people will look out for me, protect me – and you believe it.

Mick and Jen come to see you. Mick is a friend of old. He stayed with me for a while, in the big house, in another life, another past. Where I lost another part of me, four years ago. My brother in arms, my friend. When you two met, the strangest thing happened. Like clan, or kin, recognition of something. They say sheep recognise brothers and sisters. When mine returned to their flock, after two or three years, they snuffled and cuddled and had arrived home. Both of you struggled with drink and with drugs and with life. He long since recovered, you wondering and thinking, still at the maybe step, looking up. Tentatively, carefully considering a life without amber liquid warming your belly. You talked, for hours. A friend to you, a brother to us. Close and familiar despite being strangers. We sit and we talk. Honestly, openly, without soft edges or lies. Without hiding the Nothing in shadows. We talk. Mick knows about protein and weight gain. I start ordering things I have never before known. Protein powder, oats, and whey. I am not even sure what it is. And pure peanut butter. Calories, protein, oils. Retaining your muscles. Regaining some strength. You are excited. A plan. Another plan we can hold onto, follow, progress to be made. You and Mick talk quietly, I sit in the kitchen with Jen. I know what you are going to say. And how pointless it is. I am not easy to look out for. You are preparing for what I am yet to accept. Fighting talk one day and preparation the next. Confused, all I can do is to put one foot in front of the other and hope for the best. Hope not to make too many mistakes, keep you level and buy us time. After they leave, we talk about time and the future and the 'after'. I don't want the 'after', I can only deal with the 'now'. And now we have protein and green smoothies, aloe vera, morphine, and oils. You stare at me for a long time, reading and writing onto my soul. 'They are wrong,' you say, 'I feel stronger than ever.' And you blink and I know that you're lying. Not sure if to me or to you or to Us. I hold you, as tight as I dare. And I whisper, really close to your ear, 'We will fight for as long as we can. We will hold on, we will try. But, please, when it is getting too much, tell me. And we will stop. I promise, we will stop when it is getting too hard.' You nod. I do not want us to give up, as long as I can think of plans. Listen to people who have done well. Defied the odds. Why not us? But, if it becomes torture, I can and I will let you go. I promise. I will let you go.

When we, in the cottage, forged the One, the Us, we talked about absolute freedom. If you wanted to go, there was no point in staying. All we needed was trust and honesty and faithfulness. And I told you I would always be there. If I knew what you did, or thought or wanted, I could accept it and make up my mind. If I could or could not accept whatever it was, I had the right to decide.

Each of us to be free to stay with the other. Changing you was never an option. I don't change people, I don't adapt. I love or I don't. You, the first try for 28 years. You could do wrong, and you did. But changing? I did not want you to do that. I did not change for you. We grew together, forged Us. Not always easy. You struggled with my lack of demands. No changes needed, no adjustments to make. We just grew into our unit, fighting this thing today. Not a doormat, I have never been good at that. But love, unconditional, unquestioning, understanding, and whole. Safe and secure. You knew, I knew, what each other would take, accept, incorporate, or reject. That night in the cottage when you stood at the foot of the bed, and we talked about this and that and love, you said, all you knew was that you felt safe, unpressured, and well. That you felt for the first time accepted, not hiding, not pleasing. That you felt comfortable in the knowledge that I would always be waiting, at any station, at any time. And that was true. You were loved, accepted, analysed, and understood. Beautiful prism held into the light and turned to all sides. We both had bad habits, different ideas. Interesting crossovers and diverging thoughts. But from two, we became One. Protecting each other from hurt. And now, I cannot protect us from something in you. The Other, this time, is part of you. I lie on my side, you holding your small screen. Boxing, strange new obsession. Mainly Mike Tyson. I don't ask why. The noise makes me sleepy, like everything on screens. We are both winning. You watch, I sleep for a while. I do miss the news; I miss history and science on that small screen. We used to watch and debate for hours. You say your mind cannot focus, and you need simple distractions. So, I drift off, gently, to the sound of men bashing each other with leathered fists.

13

Awards

We wake up late. The sky, blue, cold, seeps into the room. Not a bad night. Only three tango trips. You managed to go to sleep late, very late. You said you liked watching me sleep. Your warrior queen at rest, preparing for another day in battle. I smile. You are a big fan of metaphors. Battle with green leafy vegetables and smoothies seems inadequate for big words. But I stroke your cheek and make my way into the kitchen. Your eyes follow me. You want to say something, but it does not reach your lips. Visitors, lovely visitors, you are looking forward to them. A call, late in the morning, scheduled, as if we have schedules left. I have some diary entries; until a few days ago, I worked from the office, but I have found that I cannot hear you. So, now, with my back to the door, I work at the table, surrounded by breaking chairs, in the front room.

There was a discussion, long before you. My twin's father was categoric. I would never have a drawing room. I was a living room person, never to be elevated to anything else. I smile back at you. They will bring wine that you will not drink. But you will raise the glass and marvel at colour and scent. Aroma for wine, I seem to remember, or is it bouquet? But I am a wine heathen without a drawing room. Definitions matter. One of my daughters, exiled from university by a pandemic, has taken up care work. We have not talked in a long time and might never again. That pain is still fresh, after nearly four years, sometimes cutting, sometimes dull. She talked to me, and gave me

61

advice, powder they use when feeding old people. Keeping alive what wants to die. Calories in a glass, easy to swallow, easy to drink. I am grateful to my young one, sharing knowledge I just don't have. I order several flavours. The nurse said I can fortify things with cream. You might not notice, and calories keep you stronger. They grade viability. I did not know that. Performance status decides if they test you or treat you. You need to score two, our reality is at best at a three, five being dead. One step up the ladder and they might reconsider. I order the powder and give you your apricot kernel. I grind, cut, mix, blend. I order, I buy, I find the best avocados, the fattest blueberries, the bloodiest beetroot. I source 100% cacao. Your eldest orders some bars. I measure aloe vera, bitter and cloudy, into shot glasses. I learn about steroids and morphine and score bedsores. The nurse gives me names, products, and sizes. I order, I cannot wait for the doctor's prescription. I learn, I am learning, please wait. I am not ready to crumble, not yet. Not for a while. You lay back, recording your voice and your face. Message of hope, feeling stronger, feeling mischievous, nothing to worry about. I stare at the crumbs on the carpet. Maybe, maybe you might be right.

You cry at the end of the call. Happy, grateful, surprise tears, big watery lakes full of honour and pride. Surprised to be honoured, surprised to be someone, to not have failed. You said, often, sober or drunk or anything in between, that you were being judged, hated, left, berated for just being you. Just being you was a curse. You could not change it; you could not do anything other than being you. Now, 'You' has become part of 'Us'. The biggest, most valuable part. I had hoped that you would come and work with me. You have so much to give. So much to share. So much to be. You carried your curse like a heavy satchel, never putting it down to rest. It now sits in a corner, next to my running shoes. Your Liberty family will remember. Every year, they will mention your name, when they reward their best member, department, worker, and colleague with the Everton Thomas award. I cry with you in pride. And, in years to come, there will still be stories about you, your high viz, your work ethic and attention to detail, your wisdom and wit. We embrace, speechless and breathless. You say you would like some diamonds, made from your ashes. One for each child, each grandchild, and three for the notice board. I nod. Beautiful diamonds are fitting. For the occasion, the memory, and your soul. We tango back to the bathroom. You remember the batteries for the scales. I promise replacement, still hoping you will forget. I don't want you to see what I see. We have survived into day eleven. I want to trap every one of them in a glass bottle, to take them with me, wherever I go. Every moment you looked at me, or at the world, with fresh eyes, with new love.

I hang a picture, where you can see it. We bought it months ago, when visiting places was still an option. We scoured charity shops, flea markets, and car boots for treasure. We bought much, investigated, researched, dismissed, archived, and kept. The picture is faded. We wanted to protect it from the sun and hid it back in your den, wrapped up, shielded, preserving the last of the glorious colours. Now I am hanging it, next to the door, where you can see the light igniting the ladies in the garden, the flowers, the children, the lovers. You are glowing, happy, content, excited. And I bask in your light. And suddenly, the light darkens, you wince, curl up, holding your precious belly. Breath heavy, painfully sallow. I rush to the bottle. A larger spoon now. You, like a bird or a chicken, open your mouth. Chickens are birds, surely. And yet they are not quite the same. They could fly, but they are shaped completely in the wrong way. Too heavy and awkward to fly, they just cluck and chuck and get fatter. So maybe not like a chicken, because you are getting thinner, and thinner, and lay no eggs. Then we breathe, together, whilst you squeeze my hand, until there is no feeling left and your knuckles are white and protruding.

Your breathing eases, your grip loosens. Pain exhausts us. We curl up under the covers until your visitors arrive and you give another performance, for them and yourself.

I do some research on your diamonds. They make diamonds from ashes now. An interesting process, quite simple it seems. It's pricey, far too expensive. At £1,700 a stone, considering that you cater for six children, their offspring and friends alike, it is unlikely to happen. I tell you. Your face falls a little. But we come up with the next best thing. I will buy small, hollow pendants on chains. Pretty and fitting and unpretentious. And give one to each of them, to carry around, to have you with them. The rest, I am to take with me on my travels. We love the idea. But the After is, hopefully, a lifetime away. And knowing that you will be remembered makes you glow and happy. Immortal in spirit, in memories and stories. Immortal as only you can be.

14

20 Kilos

A wife for 63 days. Batteries for the scales. Survivor of 12 days and nights. We are still here; we are doing well. Better than anyone thought. The nurse, impressed with your stoic expression, has earned your respect, despite her unfailingly soft voice. You dance around each other, no longer hostile, but not yet accepting. You have discovered that she can organise things we can't. Your youngest teaches me how to test blood sugars. I am not sure why, but it becomes part of the programme, our daily routine. Numbers are important, anything under 15 acceptable, under 10 good. We are now fighting for numbers, to be recorded in a small book; we are fighting for calories, for days, for times free of pain. You often forget words now. Struggling. Typing is difficult. I watch you scanning the predicted text for whatever seems to make sense. When it is getting too hard, you ask me. I am not going to type for you. We look for the letters together. It is easier for you now to record videos. You record them often, dismiss some, not liking the light, or your words. But send many. 12 days ago, we received our sentence, maybe 21 days ago, you sauntered the last time.

You stand on the scales; I catch my breath. 20 kilos in less than a month. Soon I will be able to carry you to the bathroom. You ask for Irn-Bru and four lucky dips. The man in the shop knows you are not well. He sends best wishes. Hopes you recover. Back in the car, my eyes sting, all I can pray for is a good death. Because recovery has never been an option, however hard we like to pretend. Make safe, make stable, make no worse. And if it gets worse, then let it be quick. Let it be calm and warm and happy. What does this word mean or that? I finish your sentences and you are grateful. Not irritated, not frustrated yet; you like me to understand and complete what you want to say. We are One, think as One, speak as One and walk as One. I imagine you have been a slight child. Your mother pregnant with you on her journey to England. An immigrant of sorts, born in Fulham. Arriving into a house full of uncles. The house of your nightmares. Your father's brothers and cousins. Black magic. Your small, half-Indian mother with the straight hair suffering from the cold and being unwell. Many rooms, cold, dark, damp. A fire. You remember the fire in your dreams. Unclear what happened, dreams about fear and panic and children crying. Your brother remembers a heater on fire. You remember the flames, the smell, the colours, the heat. A tall house. Not clean. Your mother escaping to church, buying flowers. Normal, she wanted normal, whatever that meant to her. You said your mother always had flowers. In vases and her garden was full of them. You later choose women with gardens. You told me how she taught you to make drinks for the bees. And you watching, the bees and the ants. A small boy in a miniature world. A beautiful boy with clean skin and old trousers.

No money to speak of and sometimes no beds. Learning came easy, acceptance not. And yet, evermore children. Nine or ten after you. You – her special boy, your father's hate festering, seeing things that might or might not have been there. Your uncle's fists and your father's, your mother's black eyes. Her retreating into places nobody could follow. You talked about her disappearing for weeks, months on end. Sometimes to leave him, sometimes to clean hospital beds. Beds to rest in, to recover some strength to return to her children, living and dead, and to bear more. Before women's refuges, before children's rights. Long before equal opportunities and 'every child matters,' she had no way to glue back together what broke in that great big house full of uncles and brothers and children without any beds. You never once asked why she stayed. You never questioned her goodness, her strength. You never said, she abandoned, neglected, did not do her best. A dream, a terrible dream, a child, a girl in her cradle, newspaper stuck in her mouth and her nose. You remember, you dream. Maybe the truth, maybe a symbol. You remember the newspaper and the fire; you remember the candles and the house with so many doors that you never found a way out. This dream came to you often, for most of your life, you said. And only the warm amber liquid would subdue it until you could no longer remember the feelings, the fear. I kiss you, remembering your dream and us talking about it. You talking, me listening, holding your hand until peace came. Comfortably numb, you called that state after half a bottle of something. Are you, now, comfortably numb? Morphine and steroids and CBD oil. Surely, it numbs that pain, too.

You gave me that little boy, you said he peeked round the corner and decided to trust. And I am glad that we had that. The boy being held and cradled and sleeping in comfort. I look at the man, in our bed, in our home, and my heart cries for the boy. He will never grow up; he will die with you in a very short time. I hope you find your mother, well and caring and loving and be her special boy. Another call, not a good one this time. Your brother, the martial artist, in hospital all on his own. His kidney, your kidney, is swollen. Tests. You ring him, in his hospital bed. He can hardly speak, but he is angry, frustrated, alone. He wants to see you. He needs to see you. He can see no point being in that hospital bed. They said he had Covid, but he himself is not sure. He wants to leave and come to be with you. Worried, he is worried, with his own health as bad as it is. You don't speak long to him. Finding it hard to hear his voice struggling, promise to ring again in the morning. You lean back in the pillows. Clean, white pillows, but ours. I bring soup that you really don't want to eat. You are polite and stare at the bowl, swirl your spoon in the hot liquid. Look at me for a long time, glassy eyes. My feet are cold, and I lean them against your legs, like always, like normal, like 12 days ago. You draw me closer, a reason to discard the bowl to the side. Rubbing my forehead, 'Don't frown, queen. It will be ok, we will be ok, we will be fine, Anton will go home and join us in talking and laughing and learning about tomorrows shrunk into todays.'

15

Green Glass

Human skin is incredibly thin. A blanket of millions of cells. It breathes, it moves, it feels and transmits, it covers, it breaks, and it heals. You say you have always healed well. The superpowers of an Emperor, a Don. Bedsores are the new front line. Drawn by the enemy in your belly as it stops you from moving around. You have not turned to the side in a long time. I miss curling up into you. You are now getting too hot under the covers; we found a new blanket for you. Fury and grey and soft, it covers your body, just. I need to find a second one, so that I can wash and exchange. You hold onto your blanket, glinting eyes. 'But I am attached to this one.' I grin, like for children, I will find an identical one. You are strong today, well. If I don't look at your arms, or your leg, or your turtle-skinned neck, you might be well, just a bit under the weather. You might venture into the other room today. I make tiny cartwheels inside. Sitting in the other room is more normal than being a Don holding court from his bed. I kiss your shoulder, cold. You ask for a shawl. One of my shawls, collected all over the world. A large one, white muslin, soft around your shoulders, making you look like Gandhi. You laugh at the thought and think of your Indian mother. We slowly dance into the other room. We bought you a cushion, a doughnut. The bedsore needs to be cared for, protected. Make safe, make no worse, maybe heal.

In the room, sitting with your laptop, your pillows, your blanket, holding court. Your family again. This time the mother of five of your children, the aunt to one. With two of the children, your youngest and the forgotten, silent one. I study his face. Kind, he has a kind chin and friendly cheeks. Eyes hidden behind glasses, but a beautiful smile. The sickly child, the silent child, prone to get lost and hide. Now, as a man, he still hides, loses himself whenever he can. The youngest one is loud, claiming possession. Claiming her place where the others just visit. I cringe, but only a little. The mother, beaten by time, fate, and destiny, dignified and still says; 'You will adjust, we all adjust in the end.' Maybe I will, but adjusting means finding something to adjust to. This thing is changing, by the day, the hour, sometimes the second. What are my adjustments to make? I leave the room and, when I return, I shrink. This is your family, these are your people, not me. Bound by childhood – you grew up in the same crescent – not far from where they all are now. Bound by pain and experience – not understood, or examined, but lived and shared. Bound by children, by a genetic future. These are your people, not me. I try to back out of the room, you see me, read behind my eyes, not fast enough to avert them in time. You stretch out your arm, your open palm looking for me.

The hairs on my arm bristle. Flee or come closer to you? Fleeing is not an option. So, I stay and sit next to you. Chatting about the weather and woodwork and gardening. She had wanted to marry you, many years ago. You let her arrange, plan, and pay for and then, on the day, you ran. As far away as you could. Stayed away for months, in fear of her brothers, who had waited at the church with her. You have been cruel, and maybe, just maybe, she still feels the pain. I try to avoid her eyes, feeling guilty, perching on the arm of your chair. Repetitive questions about my reading, yes, I have read them all. I would not dust things I don't need. Nobody notices the lovely green glass we have found at a flea market nearby. Just after Christmas I found an eye bath, exactly matching the medicine bottle. A present for you, for Us. You gave me presents, hundreds of presents over the months. You never bought me flowers, or indeed anything. In our virtual world, invented, populated by dreams, you gave me a Yak and an eagle, some quartz and some silver, a skunk and an Arabian stallion and music and pictures and crowns. You would lift your hand, closed, protecting my present, holding it over my chest, and slowly release the content into my heart. Me, a little more prosaic, hunted beautiful things for you. To come home to, to marvel at treasure and gleaming light. I lightly shake my hand away from you, make coffee and sit for a while, in the fading light on the terrace. Pondering, wondering, why did I intrude in your life?

When we met, you lived with your children, their mother, and her new husband. You rented a room. In and out you said, convenient, you said. Until the night of that terrible fight. You did not say much, just a fight, starting between you and the one with your name. Fists flailing, things being said. You said that the youngest was not your child. Hurting people, like only you can. Protecting yourself, throwing swords first. Being cold and cruel, to make them leave you, because that was all you have ever known. And yet, they are your people, your family, your history, and they should be your future, not me. Adjust, she had said, adjust. I sigh after they left and stare at you for a long time. Shall I tell you? I do, I tell you about your people and me. About me having intruded and now being caught in the glowing ashes of what was your life. You draw me closer. Holding me for a very long time. 'You are my people. You are my queen. My first home, my last home, my life.' Sighing again, I wish I could see that. I wish not to be trapped in a sticky web of other's emotions, very few good ones, all of them spilling over my heart and the carpets. And my eyes sting, burst. Tsunamis of unwanted, unwarranted tears, for you, for them, for the boy and maybe a little for me.

16

Flaccionello

14 days, the first terrible, dark, inevitable milestone. Two weeks. Maybe two weeks is better. Reaching it was paramount, important, to be aimed for, to be achieved. But it also means that from now on, we are on extra time. With the referees calling the end whenever they want. Sometimes achievements are bitter and hollow. You are proud, happy. We have been married 65 days. Lying next to you is strange, not under the same cover, the duvet suddenly too big just for me. Sliding off the bed to one side. You under the furry blanket, sweating, your head glistening in the first light. Your breath uneven, laboured, it tells me about your dream. I wonder, a new one, an old one? I slide out of bed, careful, slowly, deliberately. Sleep is important, nearly as vital as food. You do not take food, or at least not enough, I have started to note the calories down. You should have nearly 2,000, but never manage more than 800. Making safe, making no worse is growing into a chore that neither of us can manage easily. Dreaming up more and more things you might eat. You – feeling the pressure and unable to swallow. The furball in the middle of your chest, just under the diaphragm, leaves you fearful of food. You think it's a collection of mucus. I think you are wrong. You have refused to take some of the medicine. You are taking the morphine, the steroids, B12, Omega 3, and green tea. You are not taking the things that might line your stomach, protecting the lining, protecting you from digesting yourself.

I draw diagrams for breakfast, show you, use words that are new to us both. You nod. Clearly fascinated by the internal workings of you. I show you the liver, the inlets, the outlets, the functions, the possible damage, the acids escaping back into your throat. You nod again, spit into a bottle. We test your glucose – all is well in your blood. You nod again. Like drinking on empty stomachs during long, hot summer days, taking your meds without any protection might cause the furball in your chest. And you agree and now we have something else in our armour. You have some porridge with honey, and I warm some water to soothe your throat. Gallons and gallons of water. We check your heart, your kidney, your brain, your lungs, all working and in good order. Maybe, just maybe, there is a chance. You shift a little and wince. We settle, concentrating on cute animal clips. Nothing bad here, nothing at all. Today you are impatient for your visit. An important day, someone who means a lot. I need to brush hair, teeth, and make coffee. Clean the dishes away. Your half-eaten porridge. I am not mentioning it. I am not sighing, not shrugging my shoulders, just moving the dish, but you still look sad because somehow you feel as if you have failed. I turn back to kiss you.

Nothing bad is in here, no failure, no pain, no resentment. But hope is also in thin supply. Your visitors, two young men. One Australian, stocky, healthy and calm, the other one unmistakably British, tall, lanky with leaky eyes. They bring wine, expensive wine, chosen for you by someone high up. And they bring glasses. I marvel. Nobody brought glasses to drink from before. Strangely befitting gesture. You laugh, face shining and glowing. Your eyes are awake and alive. My stomach feels warm, full of happiness, grateful to them. We, Us, are happy because they love you, value you, and talk about nothing of consequence. I know that the stocky one had given you your first job after your mother died. When you were broken and ravaged and struggled yourself out of bed. You never wanted to disappoint him. And I don't think you ever did. You wanted to be superhuman for him, the lifeline for one who could have so easily drowned. They are funny, bright, full of life and fresh air. This is the moment; I am sure it is. I find the two glasses you have saved for a special day. You always said you would unwrap them when you finally had a home. Or that you would know that you had a home, because you would take them from their box. You nod, smile, and I open one box, give you the glass for them to fill. The door slams, your youngest. You gave her the key for a shopping trip. That was days ago, she has not returned it, assuming, presuming, annexing entry to our shield. I have keys for many houses, some in this country, some further away. I would never use them with the owners inside, capable of opening their own door. I have keys to feed cats, water plants, fetch mail. But never have I not knocked on anyone's door.

She wrinkles her face at the wine. Dark red, expensive, and comforting fluid in elegant glasses. Your glass is the most elegant of the three. Wispy, nearly invisible glass in your hand. Carefully twisted, turned, and sniffed. I want to tell you I love you, but don't. Squeezing your hand tighter, you read the message and lean your head against my shoulder. Sighing, happy. You have all you want. Friends, good friends, wine, a home and peace and Us. Peace for the first time, a home for the first time. You want to go to the beach. A good day, outside and in. We dress. Your clothes far too big now. I am not saying it and maybe you don't notice. Excited, ready, unsteady, but determined. They offer their arms to support you. You shrug them away, take my hand. And slowly, very slowly, we make our way up the stairs. We walk outside, in to the clean air, hazy sunshine, warm for the first time this year. Across the green, past the stage in the shape of a shell. Up to the low wall, separating the promenade from the green. You sit. We walked all the way, unsupported, unaided, just Us. We managed, under the watchful eyes of two men, who could have caught us, who keenly watched for stumbles to be on hand. I am grateful. Photos are taken, many pictures.

Your face so small, I can hardly see you inside your collar. Small, brittle, unbroken, beautiful man.

You laugh, your shoulders shake with laughter. Gladness spilling all over the beach. And so we caravan back, across the green, over the road, up the stairs and down. You, holding my hand, tightly, sometimes my arm. Secure and steady because we walk as Us. Some colour is back in your cheeks. You gleam and lighten the room, shining new light onto the tree at the bottom of our bed. Us, We, with the help of those who truly love you. Willing us on, not accepting defeat. You sink back into the pillows. Warm, happy, content. I make you some soup and you manage to eat most of the dark, caregiving liquid. Watching you is a delight. Happiness spills through the windows, clings to the curtains and flies through the air until it lands right on Us. Morphine, steroids, and vitamins, pricking your skin to record sugar, holding you as tight as I dare, we drift off into dreams, far away from Nothing.

17

Shooting Strangers

Counting up or down, measuring pain. Measuring days, hours. Measuring calories, blood counts, performance status, and weight. Measuring Us through mass and loss. Measuring footsteps, yards, and words said. Measuring and counting messages and seconds slept. A clinical life, ordered by intervals between pills and syrup, between bottles of water and bathroom trips. We have invented another way of walking. From three-legged, side by side crablike waddling, through tango, we are now a meandering train. Your arms still strong, where your legs are not. You lay your hands on my shoulder and we set off. Slowly, me guiding the way, with my hands behind me, to catch you. But you don't stumble. We don't stumble. Holding onto the bathroom wall, hands tightly holding the radiator, me sliding to sit on the bathtub rim. Both examining the exited fluid. Clear, if it is clear, your kidney is fine. We don't stagger or stumble, we sing on the way. Day fifteen of our fight with the Nothing, day 66 of married life. I dress your bedsore. Careful, the cleaning might sting. The doctor prescribed inferior cream and good dressings are not to be had on the NHS. So, I ask, learn, choose, and order. There are gold standards in dressings we did not know. Kidney and heart and bowls working fine. Your pulse fast, but CBD oil calms you enough to stay at acceptable levels. What is an acceptable pulse? Any heartbeat is surely a plus. I bury my nose in your ears. Your beautiful ears have not changed. You giggle a little and then wince.

Performance status sounds sporty, healthy, and somehow expensive. And I puzzle why five is dead and not one. I like irrational numbers, but not numbers that are irrational. Your sores are clean under the dressing but have bitten into the flesh. Not bleeding or weepy or dirty, but sore, nevertheless. You want me to take pictures, so that you can see. I do so, hand you the phone, and you look. 'Not too bad,' you say, 'good work, Admiral.' It would be better if sometimes, just sometimes, you could turn to your side. Without the dressing, airing the wound. But that is now in the same folder as me wishing you would eat more. Folders for things that we wish for, and that we can do. We concentrate for a while on astounding animal rescues. Dogs and cats and horses, half dead, transformed into show animals. It appears that love can do that. I glance at you – and why not? Why can we not come back from the brink? There are no illusions about cure and long-term plans. But mid-term can be a dream. Months rather than weeks. Your new strange need to comfort me, lying, 'we will have at least two years.' I would love that; we would love that. And I can pretend that Monday is Sunday, and we can stay here. But truth must be faced, head on, daily. Without truth, we have nothing left. We fought hard for truth, for honesty, and nothing spared. Some words were too bitter to say without bile spilling all over the sheets and cling to the air like bats. And yet, we uncovered it all. Your truths and mine. Maybe, in fairness, more yours. I had made peace with mine before Us.

Before the pandemic, whilst I still had a school, and during the summer, when you were back at work, sometimes you shouted out lyrics. On the train, with your headphones, you digested hate, bitterness, past. Those were the vodka nights. The clear fluid, burning rather than soothing. Getting you where you wanted to be, fast. Your father, your uncles, the large house, and the darkness. The death of your sister, the fire, the insults. The beatings, the hunger, the stealing, borstal, and prison. And yet, when he needed you, you tried again and again. To please, to appease, to create a new father. You were young, had a job, family, and only stole from time to time. And your father decided to be a baker. No longer a wizard, a chief, or a builder. A baker. He knew nothing of bread. He struggled and uncles and mother asked for your help. Somehow, you were always the one, who managed to give something up. You gave up time and job for your father, the baker. Three years for your mother and in the end your kidney for your sickle cell brother. Somehow, everyone else, all 13 of them, were suddenly unavoidably busy, unsuitably trained or delayed or detained. Somehow things failed for the baker, the mother, the sisters, the children, and they pointed at you. And your anger at being helplessly condemned to assist reflected in lyrics of pain and of hate. On those days, your headphones did not drown out the noise. It filled that car. It filled my heart with dread and despair. Some nights, you brought this pain into the house. Screaming and howling, shooting strangers, instead of those close and loving to you. I found out later, much later, how much you needed to hurt yourself. But you stopped when you acknowledged that you were hurting Us too. I know that anger, that helpless crying, stamping, scratching, throwing, and twisting. I know it too well but have not needed it for a very long time. The clear fluid nights were the worse. Terrible dreams, sweating, flailing. When you grew tired, I could hold you and we could breathe and soothe the small boy at your core. And in the end, he would crawl under our blanket, holding on, growing new skin. A new kind of protection, safer and warmer and good.

You bite your mouth, drawing blood. Pain and the furball take precedence over musings on music and lyrics. I stumble, my feet sleepy in the cold morning air. Our routine firmly established now. Morphine, pinprick, aloe vera, B12, Omega 3, green tea extract, apricot kernel, and stomach liner. I try to steer you away from the scales. Maybe I don't want to confirm what I see. But you need to know. Everything, every step. You have asked for your medical records. Your youngest has muddled the paperwork. Lots of signing and declaring on forms, we might have to wait six weeks. We grin. Six weeks is a lifetime. A time that we just might not have. You want to know if there is something else growing in you. You want explanations for the shadows across your lungs. I am finding it irrelevant. If they find the lungs are diseased, what does it matter? You hold onto to the fact that they call the liver a secondary. Primary unknown. Why does it matter? What will it change? But nevertheless, I chase doctors, administrators, and clerks. You want to know, that is enough. If you want to know, I will find out. You point to your breathing, laboured and stiff. You are not aware that in your sleep, your breathing is deep and even. Your thoughts make your breathing race and a struggle. And talking, talking is hard. Unknown primary is what you hold onto. Obsessive, as if someone lied to you. I call the teary oncology nurse. She will send a letter, a copy of what is on file. You want to see x-rays, CT-scans, results. I had trouble to understand the scans of my babies and am really not sure if I can tell one shadow from another. But if you wanted the Pope to pray by your bed, I would fetch him. At gunpoint if needed, for you. Make phone calls, find out, cancel work, lose work, neglect my sheep. Nothing matters, apart from bedsores, and pain and values that we might be able to change.

Your work has suggested you cash in your pension, make plans, make provisions. You will do that tomorrow, always the other tomorrow. You are chasing the primary source of your pain. And I learn about blue badges, dressings, creams, and fortified powders, suspended in coconut water and milk. You don't want any more avocado or fish, and rice has become an impossibility. But you can eat potatoes, mashed, soft and creamy. Lining your stomach with care. Our train to the bathroom reflects the four litres you drink. Mainly at night. Me, puzzling why bladders are inactive during the day. And you spit and retch into a bottle. Trying to force the furball to move. Clear fluid most of the time, until you eat. Then traces of food. The Jaffa cakes and the nuts are now abandoned, threatening treats in a bowl, waiting for you to return. Rice grains stick in your throat, so you dare not attempt them. I now have kilos and kilos of rice of every conceivable colour in the cupboard, next to endless tins of sardines. There is turmeric tea and three gingers, fortified teas for every occasion, for sleep, peace, and energy. Cupboards and cupboards of care. And nobody will ever drink all that earl grey you used to be fond of a while ago. A quiet day. Hours turning, talking, debating, researching. We laugh. We laugh quite a lot today. We are happy. And every so often, there is a minute when we forget. Forget the Nothing, the people, primary, secondary, pension pots. And we are just Us, held as one body under different covers, but lying on the same ground, the cat between our feet, talking all through the night.

18

Kale

It must be the weekend again. I can no longer tell one day from the other. Sometimes not day or night. Your eldest provides punctuation to an otherwise shapeless week. I can count the days. Sixteen today, quite an achievement, but other than that, things are hazy at best. I know some days because I have sessions and lessons online. Trying to work with my ears firmly in the other room is a bit of a task. But I can manage, and sometimes I forget, until you cough or retch. The retching tires you out. You can try for hours to bring up the furball that does not exist. My guess is that something is pressing, sideways, restricting the pipes. Internal plumbing. I study diagrams, old anatomy textbooks I have inherited years ago. My sister has become my translator. I send symptoms across the pond, and she ponders on what she can't see, but trusts my eyes and discusses, debates with her husband, also a nurse. Their prognosis bleak, like our first one. The final verdict for us is still Nothing. I tell you about her speculations, but not the sad outcomes. I don't want to be sad, I am not, most of the time. I am sad when I sit in the car. On my way to the supermarket, the health food shop, or the pharmacy. Those are the places I go. I am thankful for the pandemic, it gave us weeks to grow into Us, but also because now I can wear a mask, hiding most of my face. I am avoiding some shops. The ones where they know us, where they all ask about you. The man in the off-licence was slightly confused when he asked after you and I said you were poorly. 'Covid?' he asked, and I shook my head. 'Thank God,' he said, and I cried. Your eldest, who had once been there with me, did tell him what I wanted to keep. So, now he is sad, whenever he sees me, he is sad. And I travel further to buy cigarettes. I discover that I smoke too much. No fresh air, nothing to do with my hands. Thinking back, at the cottage, you were spitting into bottles as well. Coughing and retching, not from your stomach, your chest. I shudder. I should have insisted. Then, I should have grabbed you and taken you in. But you had said that the cough was an old one. Old pneumonia years ago. I did not know then that wives are good diagnostic tools. I tell you I am sorry; I should have been more on the ball. You shake your head, smiling, 'No Empress, it was my call.'

Your eldest arrives, all airy and bright, bringing pictures of children and health. She is talking of schools, expensive and private and the course she is taking. I know you borrowed money to help her. Paid half and for most of the books. I am glad you did. One less resentment. Something they all could agree that was good. I kiss you, your forehead, your eyes, and set off to the shops. You need T-shirts and fortified milk. Last night we talked about gripe water, maybe to settle your stomach. It needs to accept some of my care. You are resigned as I leave. Just as I enter the shop, you message. 'Where are you, will you be long?'

I rush through the aisles, take things, pick things, not knowing what. Kale, I will cook kale. Apparently, it might help. And beetroot and cream and fortified water. In the car I realise I forgot cat food, again. But I remembered your lucky dip and I'm glad. Back home, your eldest is next to you. In my bed. Your eyes wide open and panicked. I will not leave you again for more than 30 minutes, I promise, I promise my love. Visitors. I have seen them before, some of them, not all of them. Liberty family, welcome visitors. You have regained your composure, back to the clown that they know. The wise one, the smart one, the funny and outrageous one. I smile. I sit next to you on my pillows. You hold my hand. Kiss my fingers. You are gentle and happy. We have the pain under control. The washing machine chirps. It sings for attention. Finished, a good drying day. I make my excuses just for a minute. Return and my place is taken. Not sure what to do, I stand in the doorway, again, it seems to be my most favourite place. Your eldest smiles at me, gracious, and continues her conversation. Your eyes follow me as I return to the kitchen.

Chopping kale helps, I can do something useful. Layering the green strips into the slow cooker, I remember the day when we bought it. Well, not quite. You had seen that someone did slow cookers with black boards, and you know my love for chalk. We went to buy one, but they were out of stock at the time. And then, one night, not long after, you got lost on your way home. Too drunk to choose the right train carriage you wound up at an unknown place. 'I am coming,' I said, 'I am on my way. Take the next train to Three Bridges, and I will be waiting for you.' Your train was delayed, and I had some spare time. A branch of the shop nearby. I ran in and they had our slow cooker. The last one, I bought it and we sang all the way home. It now says, 'Everton's pot, stay out.' A stark warning to the cat. As a rule, he is not paying attention and lays right in front of it. Savouring smells and hoping that the lid might lift. Not that I think he wants kale, but who knows.

The visitors are gone, your eldest on her way out, I collect cups and glasses. Scanning your face. You are tired, exhausted, done. I blend a shake, with peanut butter and cream. The kale can wait until tomorrow. No hurry, we or the kale are not going away. We curl into each other. Stroking each other's shoulders. I grab the oil. Your skin is dry and thin now. The oil makes it softer and shiny. You smile, you love the smell. This is our smell now, on our skin. Seeping into us, becoming part of us. We are hoping for a good night. 16 days. We have our own new normal. Our own definition of good days and bad. Busy is redefined.

67 days married and still both hoping for a wedding night. We lay close, our hands entangled, holding on tight to each other's fingers. I notice your rings are loose. Your breath on my forehead tells me that you will not sleep. You want to fight the furball, and retch for the rest of the night.

19

Ants

Your eldest brings news of your brother. No longer in hospital. He could not stand it, wasting time, being caged in white pillows and thin blue blankets. He is at home, but not well. You try to ring, but no answer. You say you will try later again. Your eldest, close to her cousins, will update, inform, take control. She will also take control of your diary, booking that side of the family in, keeping away and invite. She brings a cousin, a brother's daughter. The brother who has made the break, got away. More hoop earrings, menacingly large. She brings a child. Confused, unhappy child. Bored, overwhelmed by the experience of beach and a thin man in his bed, speaking slowly through the tears of the women. Too early to grieve, surely. I am not ready to grieve, not yet. Your eldest will bring her children, she says, next weekend. I stare, acutely aware of my face speaking to her. No children. Please, no children. You would love to see them, I know that. And I have promised to get what you want. I will get the Pope, raise the dead, bring you whatever, whomever, whenever, but I will not bring you children. I will bring you holy water, deep sea scrolls, the Joker and Superman. But I will not bring you children. Me, your redundant protector, measuring needs against needs, cannot allow children to see your pained, sunken face. And remember a man who is not what he is, who at his core is still proud and hopeful and fighting. I place words on scales, your words spoken ten days ago. To the son with your name and the forgotten one, your youngest and me. You did not want anyone seeing the change. You wanted them to remember the clown, the wise one, the Don. You had said there would be no visitors to witness disintegration and loss. Which words do I use? The ones from that day, or the new ones? What counts? What are your wishes; really, truly, what do you want? Which part of the man has the most weight, the authority to ask me to translate wishes into reality? You said, before the lilac curtains and the nurse with the weepy eyes, you said, had you known, you would never have bound me to you. You would have retreated into a room, rented, with a bed and a chair and just waited. Alone. Your lone wolf myth, perpetuated over a lifetime of needing and hating that need. Of fear of rejection and being the first to reject. Lashing out harder, the more you loved. Hurting more the more you hit others, inviting them to hit you – hard. Fulfilling your father's early prediction.

I have to make calls, order things, really should straighten the flat. Wipe, dust, wash. Chop, blend, research. But I play with the child in the other room, whilst the cousin and your eldest weep all over our pillows. Our pillows, now a battleground, positions surrendered, willingly, with understanding, but still I have to sleep in strange smells.

You, upbeat, revelling in your newfound self, talk of years, no worries, plans to combat the Nothing and how I am your queen and your admiral. Hugs as they leave, unwanted embraces. Not hostile, but foreign, hoop earrings scratching my cheeks. Seventeen days of unpredictable changes. Seventeen days of battling pain with morphine and intruders with love. You reach for me as I again collect cups, ashtrays, and thoughts. Your spit bottle full, foamy, milky fluid, violently expelled during the night. We talk about children and visits, your face falls. I hate making you sad. But they need defending as well. Mick and Jen, they bring cake. You, serious. You want to return to the beach. For photos, memories, showing your strength. You and I dress you, easy until the socks. But we dress you, wrap you up warm. And

Mick takes one arm, and me the other. Our journey a short but arduous one. Your eldest, skilled manipulator of men, chirping behind us with Jen. Groomed, trained by her ambitious mother, a mother herself at 16. We arrive at the wall. You posing. Looking stronger than a few days ago. Swinging your leg across the wall. Normal, maybe there is more than 28 days. I count in my head. 17 days. 68 days your wife. What would I have rather, what would you prefer? 11 bad days or 9 good ones? I shake the thought off my hair, inviting sea air to cleanse me, thinking of doughnuts you owe me. I hold your arm after the photo shoot. I hate having pictures taken, run a mile and hide my face. And yet, there are posters of me, in some gallery, clad in cardboard and showing my age. We make our way back, slowly, deliberately, a blade of grass could unsteady you. People must look at us strangely. You lean into me, kiss my ear. No worries, queen, admiral, captain. No worries, we made it this far. Together, welded, meshed, entwined, Us, We, the Unit, the train to the bathroom – together we made it this far. This time, there is little glow when I settle you back into bed. You are grey, but eyes smiling in triumph. And I know that we will not see Stonehenge. So, I bring it up on Google, reality screen, sunset. Beautiful sunset that can be paused and re-played. My heart aches as you hold my hand, kiss my fingers. One by one, you hold them, kiss them, stare. My queen, my life, my soldier. Can I really not just be your wife? Your phone in your hand, reading messages. Endless messages, they feed you more than food can. They strengthen resolve that is waning. You want to go to the beach, every day, with every visitor, photo shoots, pictures depicting strength that is no longer there. We have increased the steroids. Everything works well for a few days and then needs adjusting. Never less, always more.

Now you are itching all over. Ants, you say, I have ants. I oil your skin and, for the first time, your skin moves across your flesh like ice over water. Something is missing, something has changed. From your turtle-skin neck, something has crept to your arms and your shoulder. You are hungry. I made sausage casserole with kale. The kale swims, yellowish green in the caring fluid. Two spoonsful, three, four. You message, FaceTime, try to reach your brother, I message my sister. New symptoms, what do I do about ants? Ants visited us before, and worms under your skin.

Last September. Something had spooked you. You decided not to drink anymore. You started hating the smell. And you started a journey of more pain than either of us could have ever imagined. But even then, you lied to yourself. Because you did not throw up, you thought the problem was less severe. I told you, doing this on your own was madness. Dangerous. Talk to the doctor, please, I am not equipped for seizures, vomit. But we dealt with the cramps, the ants and the worms, the sweating, the things appearing from cracks in the walls, the voices, the darkness, weakness, and pain. A week. The body requires a week. The soul needs a lifetime to shed liquid embalmed emotions and fear.

After a week, we tried to hunt treasure, ventured outside with Aly, our friend. She was confused, did not know any of it. Nothing of six days of torture. Wondering why you walked slowly and struggled for breath. You empty, devoid of strength. I watched you and held you and soaked up your sweat. I talked to the voices, weaving protective walls. Nearly, just nearly, took hold of a bottle for you, to ease your pain, soldiers choosing their battles. Baby steps. Call the doctor. You would not hear of any of it. And we survived the ants and the worms, only for them now to return. Steroid ants, are they better or worse than worms crawling under your skin? You scratch, breaking your skin. They are in your nose, under your eyelids. Oil helps, for a short while. We oil, administer steroids, morphine, stomach liners and vitamins. We talk. If we talk about them, the ants are less real. You smile, holding my chin. I drink in your eyes, willing the ants to crawl over to me and leave you alone. Nightmares to share, plans to make, days to conquer. You meditate for a while, staring at the tree at the foot of our bed. I lie still, next to you, our legs crossing each other, feeling your skin and play a game on my phone. Rescuing small furry animals is an easier task than saving your skin from crawling things. Moving colourful blocks distracts from moving boulders out of our way.

20

New Rules

Overnight, during fitful sleep and meditation, you made a decision. I kiss you. 'Good morning, my beautiful wife.' Your arm, reaching towards me; I, like a small animal, creep inside. The ants are still there, but we manage the pain. More and more morphine. I laugh – now I push drugs all day. On demand, spoons ever larger, intervals smaller. But we conquer the pain. We are ahead of one enemy, a large one at that. Pain causes stress and stress makes cells grow swifter, madder, destroying you faster. CBD oil and morphine and steroids are our soldiers, deployed with great skill. You want a hot shower. I worry about your legs. What will I do if you stumble or slip? Hit your head. 'We can manage, my queen, we can manage.' And manage we will. I prepare the bathroom, hot towels, a new T-shirt for after, coconut soap. We edge to the bathroom, unbearably slowly. Me glad, I am buying some time to prepare for slips and trips and head wounds. But you manage, in the bath, water running over your body, your shoulders. You stand, leaning against the wall. Me washing your back, carefully, soap running away into the gurgling drain. You, standing, not straight, more like a boxer, awaiting a punch. But stable. You want to adjust the taps, lean slightly and blink. And then, your first tear. Panic, wild unfettered panic. 'Help me.' What do you need? I don't understand. Do you need me to steady you, help you over the rim of the bath? No, you cannot remember which tap is hot and which one is cold. Small things, important things. You simply cannot remember, you have forgotten, misfiled the clues. I kiss you, water running all over our faces. No matter, no matter at all. And it doesn't, or maybe it does, I don't know. Holding each other's faces, under the shower, soap running over our chins. We turn the right taps, and the water runs piping hot. You smile. Conquered again, won, it did not matter at all. We can overcome everything, and we will. I sigh, we will not win in the end, but we can make days better, weeks longer, eek out time and joy. We can make little things count because the big ones are out of reach.

Back in the bedroom, our room, our sanctum, we have music and I oil your skin. Your beautiful skin. The ants have subsided, for now. They return, just as you retch into your bottle. Phlegm on the carpet, over my dress. You are not sick, it's the furball. No matter, no matter at all. You nestle back into the pillows, warm, cosy, and clean. The boy sighs, the man hunts ants on his chest. You have made a decision, you say. You want to organise visits. You love visits. You love the new role that you play, but you do feel that they steal time. Time from Us. We need time. So, visits from Monday to Thursday. The weekends for us alone. I love that, I love you, I love Us. 69 days being your wife. With the promise of 20 years. With you burying me one day. You promised, you swore, I believed you. We still have not had our wedding night. You are frustrated, I am more realistic. You marry liver disease, you know, you adjust. I kiss you, cradle your face. No matter, my darling, no matter. We will have time. You hold me as close as we dare. And I love the thought of weekends, watching the news and reading the ancients, and making plans from thin air. I ask about your eldest, your face falls. Oh, you say, I will not stop anyone coming. If they want to come, they must come. I, confused, kneel next to you. You will tell them your plan, and they will fall into line. They will understand and know what to do. Don't worry, my queen, it will be just fine. Time, we will have more time. Endless time, our time, for Us. We can sleep and eat and talk, as we have done since the beginning. Exploring each other, old and new worlds. We will have time, I am doubtful. I am not sure what the line is you want them to fall into. Nor do I believe they will.

You make a statement, public. About the new visiting rules. You start a diary, but you keep losing the page, noting down names in all the wrong orders, wrong days, and times. Lucky dip, who knows? You ask me to remember things and names you have not told me. Information without any flesh. I laugh, you laugh, we are hopeless together. And of course, the new plan will never succeed. My mind, back in the bathroom, with the taps, with your tears, wanders and wonders. Is there anything in your brain? A blockage, a clogging, rogue cells? Or is it the morphine that makes you forget everyday things? Words, I know you struggle with words, with spelling. But simple, commonplace things were easy to manage so far. Our minds meet in the haze of thoughts, the same place, same fear. You hold my face, tight, hurting my cheek. 'I am afraid, that one day I will wake up and not know who you are.' My eyes sting, sting with new pain, the grief for something I did not know I could lose. You want time, we want time, to make sure that we stay imprinted. I had never considered to lose you before our time is up. Shudder, go into the kitchen, crouch again in front of the sink, in the furthest corner from you. Hiding my stinging eyes, noise masked by the kettle. Make coffee and blend blueberries for you. You smile, wistful and crooked. Your statement made, your plan forgotten, but you remember my face. So, I am glad and ready to put one foot in front of the other, for now. The boy who never had a party when small is making the most of being a Don. You said, all weapons stay at the door. What you cannot see is there are no weapons as strong and as deadly as being dismissed, belittled, pushed gently aside, offered absorption with smiles and embraces, amalgamated, lost, drowned in noise and hoop earrings. And I am not going to tell you. For now, you remember my face and everything else – I remember for us. No matter, my darling, no matter at all.

21

Cepparello

Sun streaming through frost-clad windows. Cold outside, not yet spring. The light breaking through and we blink. Me from sleep and you from exhaustion. You avoid sleep during the night. We form our train to the bathroom, not to worry about which carriage is right and goes where. Your hands on my shoulders, following me, both singing. Me badly, you tuneless. Between us we might hit one good note. And then I notice, you notice, we notice. Yellowish spots on the carpet, tracing our way. You laugh, a little bitter. Not fast enough. Our train has too many delays, too many stops. You blame the fat controller and grin. We made it. I sit on the rim of the bath, stroking the back of your neck. Gentle, I have to be gentle. You are brittle, fragile, my precious. On the way back, we stop at the corner and hold each other. A little bit of a rest. Pricking your finger, letting the blood flow onto the small strip, gathering readings. A good morning at 5.2. Movements, routines, alien 18 short days ago are now part of normal and every day. Are part of the Us and the We. 'Good teamwork,' you say as I dispose of the sharps. Collecting small and big pills on the way. And you retch, heart-breaking, purposeful. Goading the furball. You will eat today, you say, but the furball must go. Must be purged, expelled, exorcised. I clean the carpet, pick up my cup, wander into the kitchen. Cold feet and the cat is screaming. He got here faster than me. A cigarette, I smoke more, you smoke less. And still, the noise from the bed. Painful, urgent, desperate. My coffee, your warm water. Visits today, good visits, you think. But cannot remember at all. You look at your diary, lists of things to do, people to see. Urgent, all of it urgent. Lucky dips. You sip your warm water, carefully, hesitantly, and painfully slow. Then look up and smile. 'Got it this time.' And I'm glad.

I want to try something new. A small, chalky pill for under your tongue. The nurse said it calms acids. You tried it before, did not like it, hated the taste. We tried to dissolve it in water, worse, we found, much worse indeed. I draw another diagram and show you. Explain my new theory and you nod. We place the small pill under your tongue, chalk absorbed by mouth tissue. And then you grin. The furball dissolved, ready for something to eat. You think about a big breakfast. Eggs, bacon, sausage, and something to do with cabbage. Not now, later. For now, peanut butter, blended in cream, with powder that keeps old people alive. You lean back, you will finish it later. You finished half. Half of 400 calories is 200. Not nearly enough, but a start. Protein water and aloe vera. And off to the bathroom again. Touching, moving, laughing, holding. And you speak of nappies for men. Your youngest arrives mid-morning. Flustered and sad and confused. She struggles, is angry, finding this hard. I tell her that I will stay home from now on, will just work from home. Nothing to worry about. She is angry about being shielded and not earning money. I hold her, brash, broken, unsettled girl. Heart as big as the sea but lost in the storm of life.

She sits with you talking nappies and I run to the shop at the corner. The man with the sad eyes still does not believe me and hopes to see you soon. We used to be customers of lottery tickets, tabaco, ice-cream, and whiskey. Have changed over to cat food and cigarettes. And if you remind me, three lucky dips. Quick nip into town, the Highstreet dead and deserted. There is, after all, a pandemic. I, quite frankly, don't care anymore. I find what I need, what we need and pay. They are snazzy. Grey stripes, paper and elegant. They fit like a glove. As a bonus, they hold your dressings in place. I send your youngest into the kitchen and dress your bedsores. They look good, as far as these things go. Understated with light grey stripes. You smile. Not yet. But we have them ready and that is a comfort. And the design pleases you. My medication corner is growing, we will need a bigger basket. In the kitchen, your youngest tells me about her half-empty glass. You look terrible, she thinks, and your brain worries her. Alcoholic dementia. Her verdict is clear. I remember statistics. Alcohol kills the brain. Not all in one go, in increments. And we knew that. You knew months ago, maybe years that your memory is not what it was. But you are sharp as a button. Since when are buttons sharp? Remember what you want to remember. Attention to detail is key. Protecting what is important. Everything else filed away. I hug her. It will be fine, nothing wrong with your brain that is new. You are tired and sick, but dementia? I think not. She wants me to grade your bedsore. Has it progressed to a three? No, it is fine, under control. Don't worry, we are just fine. Another coffee. You have finished your shake. 400 calories more. And tonight, you will have your breakfast. You are so looking forward to that, you grin. Mischief, you will be up to mischief. I know it and it makes me glad. A good day. The furball is under control. You feel better, we feel better. And it is still cold outside, clear, and the hydrangea sleeps for a little while more.

Just after lunchtime, the visitors. A tall, blonde one with sensitive lips, the other one, small, painfully skinny, with beautiful, clear blue eyes. One of them will be important, more important than most, but we don't know that yet. They bring a bottle of wine, and again – glasses. Chosen by your MD. Expensive, blood red, and oaky. Apparently, oak can be in wine. And cheese, lovely cheese, and sausage rolls. Strange combinations, inferior meat in pastry, delicious cheese, and wine I will not taste. You savour it with your morphine-soaked tongue.

But smile, nevertheless. You are happy, so very happy at this moment in time. We are in control of the pain, completely. You know when to ask, I know when to ready the spoon. You, tired, settle into the pillows after they all have left for the day. Still smiling, still happy. You are having a nap. Morphine and red wine, chalk dissolving under your tongue. Peaceful, beautiful face. Beautiful boy, beautiful man. I tiptoe into the kitchen, humming a little under my breath. The cat next to the sink, conversing with the fish about nothing at all. Nemo means Nobody in Greek. Nemo came to me as a refugee, left by a friend, who fled inland, because he feared a flood. Left me the fish. Eight years ago. I don't like fish, they bore me. But, nevertheless, Nemo and I somehow glide through our life, and he will just not die.

You wake, eight in the evening, darkness outside, candles, music – you smile. Open your mouth to the spoon and your breakfast arrives. Two eggs, beacon, a sausage, hash brown, and bubble and squeak. Another new concept to me. Another alien thing on a plate. But you sit up, amongst the pillows, ask me to take pictures, lots of pictures. Of you, with the cat on your shoulder, going for solid food. You don't eat it all. Best endeavours. And I try bubble and squeak. Not a bad combination at all. We return to our respective small screens, messages, you sending pictures of breakfast and you looking strong. Me, catching up with the news that I don't really take in.

22

Birds of Prey

19 days. 19 short endless days. New worlds, immigrants into new worlds, no time for exploring. Learning what's poison, what works and what we can bear. Just one foot in front of the other and smile. We have learned so much, lost so much, gained immeasurably. I hold your hand; you squeeze my fingers. Survivors, fighters of Nothing. You record messages of hope for others. After the pricking of fingers, tablets, and aloe vera, we nestle back. Warm, not under the same duvet, but warm, feet entwined. Your hands and your feet used to be cold, always cold. No longer. They are now warmer than mine. Your thoughts distant. Miss Essex upstairs on the phone. You turn to me, slowly. Serious expression holding my eyes. 'Don't worry, queen. I will make sure. I will make sure that you are looked after. I have things in place for you.' I wince. I am not easy to look after, to care for, maybe even to love. I am stubborn and torn and brittle. Get prickly when faced with care. Give, because it is easier. Taking is not one of my words. Taking is hard, accepting impossible. You know this. Although from you, with you, with us – it was easy. You were not one for making a fuss. But always afraid that something could happen to me. 'Don't drive too fast. Don't drive in the dark. Where are you? Are you ok?' Ironic, really. Very ironic and sad. It is not me who was or is in danger. It was you all along.

I wonder, if we should have known, could have known. Could have halted the process, the growth that is now unmistakably there. The swollen spot, right under your ribs. I call friends to arrange a surprise. Stonehenge now a distant dream. They have falcons and owls and an eagle. They are not far. Not as far as Stonehenge. They are happy to see us. Just ask for some bird seed. But their flying grounds are muddy at present. Too muddy for wheelchairs. They will look into options, ways to allow you to sit with the owls and the falcons. A dream, us in the desert, under the glaring white light. Looking up at the caves of Petra, falcons shriek in the air. When I was in the desert, with the hot air and the freezing sand at night, I hated it. Hated the light that hurt my eyes, hated the scorpions, hated the low, green covering in the morning, hated the sand and the rocks. But that was another life. Long before you, long before anything we now are. Long before bathroom trains and morphine, before hoop earrings and Nothing and days. Coffee, I need coffee and you want hot water. The furball is troubling again. I exchange water bottles and spit bottles with new ones. Fresh, clean, unspoiled. Recycling used to be once a week. I jolt, must take up the bins. They come early. We used to have half a bag full. Now we have three. Chip paper, teabags, empty bottles, cigarette ends, and dead flowers, remnants of visits and parcels. The nurses' plastic aprons and shields. She will come today, the nurse with the soft voice.

I have more questions, many more questions. Making safe, making no worse. How to grow back from a three to a two. Quality of life measured in numbers, scores. Like bedsores, only the numbers have opposing directions. Five dead and one is unbroken skin. Will I love you enough to recognise when you are sliding to four? Will I be able to let you go? Are you able to fight back to two? Are kale and green tea, and Omega 3 and B12 really enough? You sit up, surrounded by watery sunshine.

We look at the picture we tried to save from the light. Glorious colours. We know that the light that emblazons the greens and the reds will eventually kill them. We know, we talked about it at length. And yet, in this light, at this moment, we are happy, as happy as happy can be. Reality whooshes in with the nurse. Her soft voice unfailing. Talking and asking. Not prodding too much. I can read her eyes. You have changed. In one week, you've changed. Markedly to her. Imperceptibly to me. Have I changed? Have We changed? What has happened to Us? But I also see the compassion in her eyes. The pride of what we are trying to do. Her willing us on, giving whatever help she can. Are we, at this moment, in this place, prisoners heading for a release date, or are we condemned to wait for the firing squad? Who are we, Us, what is left apart from the bathroom train and the ever-increasing volume on spoons? Who are we, the Don and the Queen, when we are quiet inside ourselves? I snap back to the nurse and her words. She is happy to add another soldier into our army. A different kind of morphine. This will change things for the better. We have found the level for pain-free. The measures, the intervals, we know what works and how often. She offers us slow release. It means just two pills, for the morning and then at night. It means a base level of pain-free that we can maintain. It means unbroken sleep, perhaps. More than two hours at least. I don't have to top up the morphine every two hours, day and night. Controlled drugs can even us out, give us balance, a baseline. We can top up whenever we need. We shrug and hug and are happy, as happy as happy can be. Make safe, make no worse, maintain rather than fighting fires. In the afternoon, your daughter, her husband, her youngest son, and his girlfriend. Pleasant, eager, overbearing in her concern. Needs to know, for her to survive, she needs to know how many steps you have taken, how much morphine and how much food. And how about your breathing? And in the end your mood? She calls, messages, incessantly, caring. Frustrated and guilty because she cannot help. I placate, pacify, explain, and cajole. And wince every time my phone blings. You jolly along, make conversation, console until you are too exhausted to speak. You want a beach visit. The photo that proves all is well.

But you stumble when I help you into your trousers. Pictures in the garden instead. All of you, in different combinations. They insist that there will be a picture with me. I hate pictures, I tell them, you know, but nevertheless, I am put in the middle, right next to you. I don't smile on demand. If I do, I look mad, demented, and crazy. So, I just look at you from the side. Hiding my face in your shoulder, more bones now than flesh. They leave, with their care, their worry, their brash love for you. Their worry about not being around, missing the main event. Not able to give you something that you don't even need. Or maybe you do. I cannot tell. You are exhausted, pulling my shawl closer around your shoulders, shivering, cold, lost. Every day you look more like Gandhi. Mahatma, the stubborn, unyielding peacemaker, creating upheaval and pain. Unintentional murderer of children and women and men. And you, looking for peace and beauty, unaware of the toxins you invite into our bubble. The grief and the anger that swarm all around you, settling on surfaces that I cannot clean fast enough. You, attracting the bad, the flies of resentment with the rotten flesh of your liver. I straighten up things, order, wipe clean. Your eyes fixed on the picture, now in the shadows, no longer bathed in the searing light. 'Happy,' you say, 'happy and home.' And return to Mike Tyson, staggering in a small, roped world for the rest of the night.

23

Something Nice

Morning light, seagulls shouting again. They do not know or even care about human pain. Food sources in the shape of tourists. Locals know better than to eat on the beach. Twenty days, 71 days of married life. The cat, sleepy, stretches, his claw stuck to the blanket. You, wide awake. Last night, morphine, less than every two hours, in-between bathroom sorties. I am grateful, my twins have taught me not to need sleep. They never slept for two years, at least not together or at the same time. Trained insomnia, strengthened by my friend PTSD. Once, I stumble a bit, trip over the carpet. 'Be careful, my love, watch out.' During the night, talking and talking, we stumble across an idea. Kaftans, kaftans are loose and long. They will cover your legs. Less scary for people to see. And I explore and compare, show you patterns and sizes and lengths. You laugh, my eagerness makes you chuckle. You say you want lamb for Easter. My eyes sting. I have become dishonest with you. I cry in the garden, a long way away. I agree to lamb for Easter, discussing how to cook, how to serve – knowing, guessing, suspecting, that there will be no Easter for Us this year. The twins also taught me about stockpiles. You need more than you think – of everything. So, I order three kaftans, despite the fact that we have only one body to dress. One pink. Stripey, one dark blue and white, and the one we both love equally, long, flowing, desert colours all the way to the floor. You say you will leave the bed more, see visitors in the other room. I am glad, leaving the bed is a two. Self-care and being

101

bedbound are yardsticks when measuring quality. How can anyone measure quality of life? Do you have quality? Do we have quality? I am not sure what that means, but we do have life. And we hold onto the breathing, the pulse, the numbers, the weapons, the smiles and the laughter, bad jokes about nappies and bathroom trains. We hold onto me being able to work in the other room, sometimes, because it pleases you to hear my voices.

You want Normal around you, whatever that is. In our way, we attend training together. Zoom with background, muted mikes. Both of us issuing verdicts on trainers and trainees alike. Tonight, I teach a whole class. German for adult beginners. The new world order has brought people together like nothing has ever before. From Cardiff and London and everywhere else. Stories, and backgrounds diverse, collect on my screen, with you listening and smiling. Is that the quality in our life? I cannot be sure, but I know that this is Our quality and Our life. Visitors today, lucky dip, because you cannot remember. I have to collect our new morphine pills. There are many of them, visitors. I don't really know who sits where. The pharmacy has no knowledge of our new soldier. Between the doors of the pharmacy and the surgery, I stumble. Tired, incredibly tired.

We need this new soldier to sleep. The girl at reception, after a thousand questions, about mask, Covid symptoms, and relationship, buzzes me in. My eyes frighten her. She searches and searches, but nothing. I go to the car, ringing the hospice, they assure me all has been done. But they will do it again, now. They press the button. And back to the buzzer. The girl shrugs. She is sympathetic with helpful hands and a cheery manner. She searches the screen. Nothing. A word I am best friends with by now. Nothing. But because of my wild eyes, she will try something else. Bring someone down from Prescribing. Maybe they can see different things. And as fate wants it. My friend with the overblown sense of importance, who works in the office, prescribes, is summoned. 'Where is the lady?' and then stares at me, blank and then comprehending. Tears, please, do not cry all over the counter, or me. She says that she is sorry, or something to that effect. Asks if I am happy for her to help and I nod, twice. She finds the prescription and I can see that she is going to say that the doctor will sign it later. For me to come back. She hesitates for a split second and leaves. Returns with the script, opens the flap in the counter, takes my arm and I follow her into the pharmacy. She tells me again that she did not know, that she will lock files. Something about unethical and involvement. I nod, not listening, unhearing, uncaring. The pharmacist asks if I am sure that I want this strength, that there was no mistake. No mistake. 30 pills, 15 days of potential sleep and no pain. I take them, thank them, and stumble home. I send her a message, apologise for the surprise. She answers, sad, and tells me that she cannot offer support. I am puzzled and slightly offended. Cannot recall having asked for anything but the pills. I show you the message, looking for a translation. You type an answer to her.

In our room, around our bed, visitors, too many of them. You on the phone, laughing, discussion on football and whatever else. Happy, you are happy, and everyone nods. I go to the kitchen, your youngest is there. I ask whom you are talking to. 'The bank,' she says. 'Some manager,' because you want to make a number of large transferrals. Surprised, I take my coffee and sit next to you. You take everyone's details, relate them over the phone. Nod, laugh, happy. Big presents, you say to the man. Grandchildren, your children, their mother, your youngest. 'Buy yourself something nice.' The Don, the boss, all it needs is them kissing your rings. You revel, you bathe in light and generosity, this time your own. Your mother's estate has come through. You, who had hoped that there would be nothing. To spite your siblings, to wreak revenge for three years of care in a prison of tea and white curtains. To be judged in the end when you, tired and broken, were blamed for whatever entered their minds.

You had been away for a long time. Came back when the call came. When nobody was available, or capable, or willing. To take care of the mother who could not take care of the boy. And strangely as well, in a roundabout way, for the father you hated and who hated you more. Because he was there, too, for a year. Dark times, dark days, cabal, and conspiracy in your mother's front room. She knew nothing of it, you are sure. Small, confused, lost mother with the straight Indian hair. And then they came back, with wide open hands, looking and searching, demanding, and taking and pushing you to one side. You, angry, defeated, stood far aside when they buried her. Talked to her later, quietly, on your own. And you wanted the lawyers to squander every penny they wanted to fight over. But now, three, four years later, you have received your share. At last, that fight is over, and you can be the Don in his bed, disposing, giving, bringer of wealth, as small as it is. They leave and I hold your shoulders, we stare at your mother's cross. You want me to keep that, take it with me, wherever I go. You want your mother to travel with me. My cheek against yours. Wet streaming from your eyes. The last fight over, the last redemption achieved. I don't ask anything; it is not my place. What I don't know yet, what I will know later, is that the story is going to be repeated. Your care and love for your mother, you, being edited out, maligned, tarnished, dismissed, pushed aside, and judged. All this is going to be repeated, in deeds, in words, in pain – later when you leave me to fight for you and for Us. After, later. And if you knew now, would you change anything? Can history, destiny, faith, and calling really be changed? But we know nothing of this, not yet.

24

Leap Years

I have always struggled with the seven times table. But today, we had 21 days. Three weeks since the first day. 72 days being your wife. And now, after the first dose last night, we have morphine as pills, only administered twice a day. With top-ups if needed. There is still no ceiling on morphine. But we are evenly, sustainably without pain. You are happy, feel stronger, try to walk on your own. I will you on, cheer silently for your success. And you triumph. Surely, we have scored some points. The greatest common factor of 21 and 72 is three. My brain wandering, searching for patterns, for no reason at all. 7,305 days you promised, we promised, we planned for. We had 72. And if the doctors are right, we might only have seven more. Leap years, I smile.

After we met, very soon after, you talked about leap years. Every night, in the kitchen, you talked about leap years and that I could ask you to marry me. You said the warehouse people were teasing you, daily. They said you were in love and, with it being a leap year to come, I should ask you. I laughed. You held me in the small cottage kitchen, with the cat getting under our feet. You were insistent, drunk or sober. The same conversation. In the end. I asked what you would say if I were to ask. You kissed me and said of course you would say yes. I was happy at your smile, smiled back. But asking you was not my style, and you knew this. So, we danced around each other for several weeks. The same conversation, night after night. You did not ask, nor did I. Each of us proud and independent. Each of us frightened, excited, and maybe a little bit hopeful. And so it went on, before we left the cottage and I lost my school and we forged Us. You relayed conversations with grown men from work who told you, you loved me and were happy and safe. Who told you my cooking meant something bigger than food. I did not believe that any of this was said. Not in a warehouse full of wine and men. But you told me; tried to convince me and marvelled. The cottage was small, shaped like a long boat. Stuffed with books and pictures and my heavenly space. Just mine. Until you, until Us. Outside of the window, in a small window box, that year, one daffodil bloomed before any other and lasted for several months. It withstood storms and rain and frost. And we called it the Everton. The box and the flower are outside our new kitchen window. But I have not seen the Everton yet.

Everton is an old Saxon word, meaning wild boar from the forest. I would prefer it to mean something else. You sweated a lot last night, but no pain. Your forehead is clammy, the sheets stiff. But you walked, alone, to the bathroom. You did not need the singing, talking, walking stick that is me. I am happy. You are proud. Little things. Little things matter. Your granddaughter has brought a picture of her son and a card he had made.

I made a frame and for the first time you wanted a photograph of the family up on the wall. Where you could see it. Your great-grandson. I am glad. I am glad that I can do that for you, for Us. You want a book. A book for people to sign and write something on every visit. 'New rules' you say, 'they have to sign the book. Go to the beach with me for pictures. And nobody after Thursdays.' I find a book, carried with me for many years, bought in Malaysia, for no purpose at all. Pretty, black velvet, silver stitching gleaming with hope and with pride. I find it with unexpected ease. When we unpacked the boxes last summer, you ordered books according to size, not purpose or theme. It still irritates me, but ordering things is not a priority, not yet, not then, maybe not ever. Maybe, when all this is over, and you leave me, I will give them away. My books, like children, I cling to them, clung to them for so long. But when there is no longer an Us, I might have to let them go. Senseless, because I will have lost my purpose, and too heavy for rucksacks and running shoes. And they are, most of them, imprinted in me, with indelible ink. Some, I could read to you from my mind. You love books, you said. But reading with cataracts and a brain full of whiskey is tiring at best. You told me that you had been sober for several years. Looking after your mother required attention and tea. But when she died, you found in a room, where your father's things were, several bottles of rum. Lined up, waiting for you and your liver. You sat in her chair, staring out of the window, and swallowed and swallowed and slept. You believed that men should not cry. Emotions considered as toxic, dangerous, painful things. Unordered details to be dismissed. You stayed in that house, for weeks, for months, until the others, your brothers and sisters, thought it was time for you to move on. Not a home, but a place. Full of memories you tried to forget. Your mother's house, your mother's chair, but your father's rum to sustain you. You had given up work because nobody else could or would or felt equipped. So, once again, it was you. Dark, sweet, full-bodied Jamaican rum. And when that ran out, whatever came handy. As bottles or powders or pills. During that time, unspeakable things. Just to hurt you, you needed pain to feel anything. I found the pictures, the videos. You gave them to me, with your laptop, the password. And I watched, vomiting, crying, and wanting to hold you and hit you at the same time. There is resentment, I told you, there is some of that. Other women had time, laughter, your skin in a way that destroyed you. You had fun with others, and we are paying the price. You held me that day, very tightly, and kissed my resentment away. You said you were sorry, but there was no way you could have foreseen Us.

A different life, away from memories and failure, from pain, being misunderstood and judged. A life that you wanted and that wanted you. A future, a dream. Someone to be there at every station, every time and feed you and care.

You go and sit in the other room for a while. Stripping the bed, I cry for a bit. Not angry, resentful, just sad. Sad for you and for us. And sad for my books that I might have to let go. And sad for your mother, your brothers and sisters, your children. Just sad. After changing the sheets, I sit with you. Not many visitors today, just Us for a while. Leona, dear, weary Leona, my friend for many years, sits opposite us for a while. She is honest and sad, sensitive and experienced. Her fight with the bottle, decades long, still at the half-winning stage. Not quite won, not quite conquered. She tried to support, last summer talking to you. Understanding, loving, suffering, mainly sober Leona. In the end, she translated to me some things that were alien. Me, child of an alcoholic, a violent one to boot. Running pubs, owning one, drinking for work, but not to forget, I had never imagined that I could love a soul coated in amber fluid. Not like this, not as part of my being. I watch you; you are growing tired. Time for this evening's morphine. A good day. No pain, not bedridden. I think there is some quality in our life.

25

Hot Chocolate

The new rules disbanded, discarded, forgotten. But I did not expect anything else. Rules and plans are there to be made and ignored. We have plans for eating, for sleeping, for the shape of our days. Plans for walks and the future. Plans for writing and reading, for poems, and I made some secret plans for falcons and owls. Three years ago, I had made a plan. A good plan, viable, life changing, funded, calculated, worked out every detail. Hope. And we worked hard, Sue and I and later Hayley. We worked so hard for the dream. No money earned, no salary, no wages for 12 months. We wanted different, better, holistic. We wanted and could change the world. And then you came. I kidnapped you. We forged and invented the One. After five years of working together, having each other's back. Old prejudices came to the surface and drowned every plan in their path. After our weekend, the kidnap, the talking, the holding, the knowing, the Us, I met them on Monday morning. Glowing, happy, and showed them a picture of you. And suddenly, ice-cubes rained from the ceiling in Hayley's new house. Spitting of hate, unreserved and undeserved. Criminal, low-life, and never to come near our school. Me, baffled and battered by words, deflated, confused and alone, spat back like never before. Of course, we patched up, soldiering forward. Me painting, them doing the office work. Careful not to break nails. The golden moment, the opening, cheapened by stupid balloons. And you, amongst them, drunk and alone, accepting and wise, listening and taking in. We had spoken about me lasting a couple of years, us buying a house, saving some money and me jumping ship to go it alone. I hoped for us to share it, eventually, the work, the purpose. You had all the skills, all the experience required. In a way, you could give far more than me. First students, back at the board after so long. Happy, so happy, having it all. Getting paid, us buying a frivolous ice-cream. You wistful, Sue spitting and plotting at Us. And then she found reason, mistakes that were never made. And then, now a year ago, there was nothing, but some compensation and bitter taste in my mouth. Really quite a short story, but the end of a dream, the big dream for me. You cursed them, angry and sad. You wished on them death and destruction and drank more and more. But maybe that was only because we had more time. First lockdown. Endless days talking and eating in bed. And talking and planning and hoping and forging Us. Finding each other. Solace and ice-cream and Madame Butterfly. We were happy. The cottage bathed in the sun, a glowing dome of protection. The money would last for a while, and I would find somewhere else.

Protein shakes and yogurt, beetroot, green tea extract. CBD oil and protein-rich water. We have an assortment of pills. We love the small pink ones. The slow-release morphine, they buy us more of the nights. You snore gently, or me, in turns and sometimes together. You don't like the dark anymore. Some of your dreams are back. You dream of being cocooned, hanging from somewhere up high. Together, with hundreds of others, waiting for something, unsure what it is. And then falling, leaving your pupae behind. There is nothing after the falling, apart from the cries of a child. You hold onto me. Frightened and lost. I make coffee, warm water, and boil an egg. You suddenly ask for hot chocolate. It has to be from a special tin. Just like your mother liked it. Heat milk, stir, heat again. I will go later and find it. Hot chocolate has calories and milk is like food. 22 days into our journeys, new tastes, new needs, small things that matter. 73 days of learning to be your wife. Closer to deadlines and something neither of us understand. We are prepared, we talk, we wonder, but neither of us knows. We don't understand the details, reality is speculation at best. And maybe that is a blessing. We are, in many ways, blessed. We are warm, have a home, have friends who bring wine. The cat and the fish are ok. We have pills and nurses and phones to pick up when I don't understand. We have videos to share with others, messages can be sent. We can source, order, and buy things that we need. We have the sea outside of our window, listen to storms from our shelter. We are protecting each other. In so many ways, we are blessed.

Your sister, your gentle, beautiful sister, holding your hand for a while. Finder and bringer of peace. Your father destroyed her spirit, you say, with his dark magic and entangling her. She was beautiful once, in a more obvious way. He saw an asset and blew her mind. That, and genetics, I am sure. She talked to you, often, over the phone. She said that your father had loved you, on speaker, so I could hear her voice. You shrugged, feeling anger and hate, but never shared that with her. Your beautiful, delicate sister, holding your hand now, bringing you peace. I love her for that. I am glad she is with us. After she leaves, with her Irish companion, your eldest rushes and gushes in. She used to come Saturday mornings, but has now extended her stays. The B&B a few buildings away, with the fourposter bed and the sea view, is her new home for the weekends. Your eldest, who embezzled money, stole savings to pay for her wedding. Your eldest, silver-tongued and golden-eyed, makes mint tea in the kitchen. The cat watching her, sad. Whilst I am making your chocolate, she sidles up closer to you. Back on my pillow, spreading her smell over the sheets. Seeping into the walls, creeping into my bones. Holding her phone to your face, talking to her children, smoothly and happy and save. I sigh and sit in the other room. Working my way through other's pain. They don't know, the people I work with, what is in the room behind. My secret for now. And for a moment, for the briefest of moments. I am absorbed and forget.

26

Shadows

We are still here, my new mantra. We are still here and safe. Nothing bad happened or will happen – yet. Maybe it never will. Maybe the pills and the tonics, the kale and tomatoes and apricot kernels have bought us more time. The windows are always open, fresh air, salty air, some find it cold. Routines are embedded, we know what to do. The pills, vitamins, and aloe vera. Then shakes, and then pricking your finger, collecting your blood. I bought you a smaller tumbler, with a bright green palm tree lid. Sometimes a big glass of protein shake scares you. Smaller portions are easy to swallow, easy to keep. Water, you drink gallons of water. But you can walk on your own. Unaided, most of the time. With me in attendance only in case and because we usually walk as a pair. You stroke my cheek, smiling. My Queen, my dear Admiral. The mornings and the late nights are still ours. Belong just to Us. Keep us sane. Selfish time, our time, regaining strength time. Your breath on my ear is warm. I study livers and blood vessels. Furballs and outlandish cures. We discuss, consider, dismiss. My friend has offered a shaman ceremony. You laugh, cannot imagine a shaman from Brighton, dancing around the bed, curing lesions, regrowing livers, and healing lungs, by swinging feathers and chants. We draw the line at some things and research others more seriously.

I noticed last night a change on your skin. There are new strange dimples and cuts. I have seen them before, on others, sinister growth. There are two on your face, and some on your chest. I know you noticed them, too. But we do not discuss those. Some things are better ignored. Your skin, looser and looser; oiled though and smelling divine. The bedsores, although not healing, are under control, dressed and clean. Your voice, your beautiful voice, is changing. Whispering, hoarse, sometimes painful to hear. You rest it as much as you can. Nobody shall notice that you are losing your strength. Your blood is still clotting, your eyes are bright, temperature normal, heartbeat steady and strong, urine clear like water. There is not much wrong with you. In our hearts, we know the illusions, we know the ultimate sentence. But something in us is upbeat today. You are excited, order a skull shaver, to groom, to feel better. I add honey to all your hot drinks, in the hope to soothe your throat. You mentioned the shadow again, they found it on your lung and somewhere near the trachea. We are still waiting to see the pictures, the medical records not yet released. I suggest we contact your surgeon, the one that has seen inside you, removed a kidney, and told you to lay off the alcohol. Maybe, just maybe, she could translate the pictures, the words and help us to find a new plan. You, hesitant, but willing, will contact her as soon as you can. You are busy studying form for Cheltenham. And I stitch together a picture of human anatomy. Functions and what can the body withstand. A new pain, irritating. Right shoulder is hard to move. You think your lungs are not working. Your breathing laboured and painful. However, when you are sleeping, deeply and save, your breathing is fine. I know anxiety breathing. And I find out that the liver, when just about ready to go, sends pain signals into right shoulders. A new wonder weapon, I have in the bathroom. Easy to use. Deep Freeze, with added pain killers. You sigh. All better. But you also ask for more, extra Paracetamol on top of the morphine. We develop new scales. A pain scale, from one to five, five being the worst. And a wellbeing one, with 10 just outstanding and two barely bearable. So, whenever you need to tell me, or I simply need to know, you issue me with numbers.

A code, secret and significant. You are happy at eight. Eight is a good day. We don't want to slump under five. And pain exceeding 2.5 requires attention. Your memory, hazy, cannot recall anything you have heard a few hours ago. Visitors, things to do, things discussed with others and words, often words disappear in your wonderful brain. The good news, the ants have moved on. The retching up furballs is now a permanent feature. I am sure you are making things worse. You force and you force until phlegm spills into the bottle, over the floor, the covers, your feet.

After 23 days of plans, revised plans, new plans, facing invisible enemies, grappling with demons, some yours and some mine; after 23 days of looking for a stable, manageable space, where we can rest for a moment, assess, evaluate, regroup, your body still finds surprises for us. No day without change. Without new ways to torture the already tortured souls. We talk about endings, the After. Sometimes dismissing, sometimes staring directly at truths that cannot be changed. And sometimes, there are moments of hope, of something untouchable in Us. Sometimes, you can walk and talk like before. Your mind clear and bristling with mischief and love. 'Cheltenham,' you say, 'we will make Cheltenham.' And I smile, a betting man. Part of your plan for my future is a big win and a ten-year lottery ticket. We hold each other. Your shoulder now in less pain. We have dealt with the pain, the ants, sugar levels, paper curtains, and bitter cold. The furball is stubbornly present, your retching part of the background noise. Your eldest, for the first time confused and unsure. We are waiting for the kettle to boil, for your warm water and her mint tea. She has news from your brother. Back in hospital, in an induced coma. He could not take oxygen through a mask. His breathing controlled by machines. She does not know how and if she should tell you. I think you ought to know. And something in me thinks that you know already, connected by kidneys as you are. I tell you, with her sitting still. You close your eyes for a moment. There will be no tears in front of your eldest. You sit up and begin our day.

27

Male Model

The last day of the month, does that count, does it matter? Your eldest bemoaning being so lost. None of her siblings talking to her. Not her sibling-cousins from your side, nor those by her mother. But she has what she calls 'the cousins'. I have no idea who they are. You told me, how she wanted better than you. How you never quite measured up to her friends, her world. And how then, years later, she needed you as her witness in court. To say what, precisely? You did not know. You were hardly first-hand, not even second. People kept whatever it was from you. And you, knowing you were not guilty, but being judged, nevertheless. You, confused, angry beyond words. Could do nothing to undo the past. You thought her guilty herself, blamed her, called her knowing, manipulating. I argued for the child that she was. Even later, when she went off the rails. Thinking about it, all your children, confused, neglected, loved unloved children, like you, became creators of their own hell. Easier to create your own hell than remain in the one prescribed, laid out and dictated to you. Better to have some control. Not real control, but perceived. I know that I build many of those over time.

Cold, unspeakably cold in our room. The daughter with too many worries, sending relentless messages. Wanting to know answers. Wanting to know how you are. Your youngest bought furniture and is building tables at home. Sending pictures, proud, accomplished. She will make soup for us. Your boys, your sons, remain silent. The silent, forgotten one, comes with his mother or brother, never alone. He is fragile, smart, and unhealthy. I want to hold him, render him visible, give him a voice. The very eldest boy, trustworthy and honest, upright and stoned, hides tears whenever he sees you, looks strong in his fragile state. And the one with your name, after his visits, calls twice. He knows he is most like you and that scares him. Safer for him to stay away, to keep distance, created by words, by time, by absences and presences. You wanted him to take over from you, as my protector against the world. But we both know the impossibility. He can hardly look after himself. You disapprove of his choices. You cannot understand why he is not walking away from his child. Thinking he is inviting more pain. And he is, but he does not want to be you. He rather sleeps in his car. To be near, available, touchable. And I respect him for that. You don't, you condemn him. Thinking him weak again. And he winces under unspoken words. Hurt, angry, confused, and alone. The man of the house, his mother's house when you left. Displaced by another, whom his mother now hates, but has to care for, a cripple by all accounts. Putrid, stale air in all rooms. He, again, lives with his mother, his brother, and for a long time you. All lodging in rooms without beauty, without air.

Things have been said, over the years. Horrible, wounding things, between you and your children, and all of you have grown thorns. And their mother, stoic, dignified mother, has created a myth. Trying to melt the unmealtable into one golden pot. 'We are a close family.' You slept for most of the way, that day, when you moved from the darkness towards the turquoise green sea. And then, at the end, shouted at waves and the savage sky. Alive, We were alive, Us free of shackles, with a future ahead.

Your eldest speaking about her children to you. Mellowed, calmer; I feel for a little girl. Embrace her on her way out. Back to the fourposter bed, assignments to write for the course that you, who were not good enough to break bread with her friends, to bring her up, had taken a loan out to pay. You laugh, you have an idea. Strong enough to walk to the other room. I am metric, know nothing about yards and feet. But I guess you walk ten metres, modelling nappies for men. Grey striped, classic design. I video you walking and twirling, as far as your body allows. You are right, things need to be out in the open. Stigmas dispelled and laughed away. Clad in my white shawl, mischievous, gregarious, free of pain. And when I stop filming, the show down and dusted, wrapped, ready for you to edit, you lean on me. Deflated, tired, but laughing and proud. You want them to know, all of them, the friends and the children and everyone else, that nothing can beat us. Challenges accepted by Us, by the team. I silently pray for your brother and his breathing machine. Unclear if it is the pandemic, the kidney, or sickle cells. But something is fighting within him, fighting to see you. And I will strength his way. I want him to live, to succeed, to get well. Somehow the two, the brothers are inextricably linked. Linked by time, pain, and kidneys. I worry, I pray and despair. You edit your film and send it into the world. The modelling complete, illusions made public. But a message of hope, to the Us and the world. I kiss you, gently, and fetch you a yogurt with 300 calories.

28

Poems and Mattresses

We all have quotas, one way or the other. Of heartbeats, smiles, embraces, mistakes. But never knowing when they run out seems unfair. Negotiating into the dark, stumbling and stabbing at nobody knows what. Collecting pictures and meaning. Memories locked into cells that slowly disintegrate. I am grateful, glad, that you this morning, like on all others so far, remember my face. We are at the beginning, a new month, Spring soon. You, more tired than usual, defer food for later. I frown. What makes you not want to eat? What fear stops you from accepting warmth and strength and care? You make efforts in many directions, but not sticking to any plan. Messages, your new addiction. You need to see responses, be reminded that you still matter. Not forgotten, still with a purpose. For me, for now, it is enough that you still remember my face. My face in your hands, your eyes in my eyes. Sweat pouring down your skin, collects in new folds. I open the window. The V-shaped pillow arrives. You wear it, wherever you go. A dinosaur on tiny legs, moving from bed to chair and from chair to bed. Aided by an insignificant queen.

I shrink, have shrunk for some time. Into the walls, the pills, the blender. Me, whose hair used to arrive in a room before me, fading now into the afternoon haze. The nurse with the soft voice, concerned. There are things she can order, arrange, do from a distance. Your bedsores score well. They are not healing, but they are no worse than last week. She takes me to one side, quietly, dignified, unruffled, unpanicked, concerned. She has seen more changes. You have lost more weight. Your skin has changed colour. More sallow, slightly yellow in tint. I know, I can see, every day I can see. But closing my eyes brings more peace. She holds my shoulder and is the first to ask: 'What about you?' Startled, I step back from her hand. There is no Me outside Us. She will order a mattress topper and a cushion for your chair. Easing the pressure on your skin, they should help to make safe, prevent further damage. And maybe my dressing and creaming and caring can heal a bit of your skin. Poems, I am writing more poems for you. I want to make you immortal, make Us count for something that cannot be taken away. Poetry, there is no poetry in this thing that is going to take you away. But there are poetry and beauty in our train to the bathroom, in rubbing oil into your skin, in your eyes and maybe, a little, in a hope that has no basis at all.

You will not be able to see the falcons, the ground too wet, too unstable.

Nobody wants you to fall, in front of the birds. Me, working in the next room, teaching, pretending. Willing another reality.

Today, it is quiet. We are quiet, no furballs, no ants. Pain under control, you study form for Cheltenham, our next goal. Not quite. But there is no reason to think that we cannot make 28 days. Back in the cottage, horse races, we had already packed up, not sure where to go, but needing to do something productive. Something practical, something real. We, entwined in each other, followed the hoofs down the green. You, as always, a gambler, a betting man. Me, not ever having staked anything on a chance. Apart from important decisions, for those I will throw a dice. I choose horses by name or by colour. Mine came good more often than yours. We laughed. Your bottle was empty. I walked to the Coop in town. A bottle a day, then. I did not mind. Did not worry about money or consequences, became your aider, abetter. Giving you sleep without dreams. Making you comfortably numb. I wondered if you needed the fluid, the liquid, the amber, to make me appear pretty and suitable. You held me, tight, and shook your head. 'I love you, my darling, my soon-to-be wife.' And I believed you. I felt you, smelled you, your grip was steady and warm. You said that you loved me sober, or drunk or anything in between. And I loved you, more than the sea and the beach and the sheep. But who can be certain of anything? What happened to Us? To our peace? Swallowed in foreign toxins, in mad cells and dying hope. Swallowed in past misdemeanours, in memories I do not share. Swallowed and drowning and lonely. I wish I could take to drink. For us to go back, six months, a year. Different decisions, the doctor, some help. Treatment, options, any kind of option. I even would be glad to let you go, back to your old world, back to whatever excitement it was. If you just live. Knowing that you are happy wherever, would make me glad.

I had asked you, back in the cottage, if you wanted to return to that other life. For a day, a weekend, forever. Fearing to bore you with my poems, my pictures, my flowers. You looked at me strangely, focusing hard. 'No, there is a lifetime exploring to come. I will never tire, never feel bored. There is so much to learn, so much to see. I found my Queen, my Rock.' No, you wanted this, Us, the cottage, a home and even the cat. We twirled and whirled around rabbit holes full of treasure, we danced around demons and fears. We forged an army with unbeatable strength. A force with power, unbeatable power, conquering everything in our path. And all the while, we did not know, the creeping, seeping shadow in you. 25 days ago, we saw it, the shadow, we were told it was real, your worse fear, my ending. 25 short endless days. A lifetime swallowed in morphine, measuring, evaluating, recording, pills of every colour and size, researching, visitors, bathroom trains, and green tea extract mixed with CBD oil. The kitchen is full of the remnants of plans we will never fulfil. Rice in all colours, all manners of tea, vegetable, fruit and smoothies, hot chocolate, cream, broth, and soup. Maybe, just maybe, we should stop fighting, looking for options that are not real, and love and enjoy the moments we have.

29

Yam

26 days into our journey, 77 days your wife. We have found some routines; some things are familiar. We start the day with the pinprick, recording just for recording's sake. It would not make much difference, but it is something to hold onto, practical, real. Measuring glucose, aloe vera, and pills. Dressing your bedsore, strangely pleased at the sight that remains static, not healing, but not getting worse. The hope you might eat. You try every so often, a little, I fear, just to please me. The messages, videos, keeping the hero alive. No news from your brother. Me changing the sheets, you, sitting on the throne of your new cushion, next door. Donning your kaftan, the desert striped one, looking regal and fragile and unbreakable. Your moves from the bed to the chair, strategically planned. You need your laptop, your tablet, your phone, the bottles for water and spit. Your diary and your pens, tabaco, ashtray, CBD oil, and socks.

Sometimes you get impatient. I know what the list contains. But sometimes, just sometimes, you forget that I know. Remind me when there is really no need. You say that you are surprised, how patient you are with being a patient. That there is never the wish to explode, to be rude or abrasive. You tell me about a time, in that other world, when your middle daughter found you in the dead of night. Stabbed, bleeding after some kind of business you would not explain. She tried to patch you up in the bathroom, too young, too frightened, I'm sure. And you shouted at her, she was not fast enough, not efficient enough. You hated not being able to rely on yourself. Unfair, you know that; she was just trying to help. And she is prone to panic, to flap and worry. You remember that day and regret floods into your eyes. But you will not say it to her. I will tell her later; how sorry you are. How truly sorry for rejecting her care. I am surprised at the ease with which we accepted and took on our new roles. The Us, the We, finding a balance of care and fighting, of stubbornness and love, of laughter and fear. No panic, no flapping, just one foot in front of the other. I kiss you. You will love the new mattress. Delivered whilst you hold your court. I use the white duvet cover, our favourite, seldom used because time to iron and starch is in thin supply, and you often spew phlegm around our bed. You hold my hand for a very long time, pull me to sit on the arm of your chair. Your sister, your soft, gentle sister brings yam and ackee in tins. I tried to cook yam once, still not sure what to do. But I will try. I made pineapple cakes for you, for Christmas, and you were polite. The same Christmas I ordered a fountain pen from Harrods. You had mentioned that once you had a beautiful fountain pen. You mentioned a man with a big house, stuffed to the rafters with treasure. He gave you the pen, eventually, it got lost and you grieved. You love treasure, we collected plenty. Weekends spent searching, buying, and then researching over coffee and rum. We made a theoretical fortune. I reality, we just have more pretty things. Like most of my presents, you kept them, locked, unused in the drawer.

Things I might not need very much longer. When the Us, the We disintegrates, what will become of me? I shoo the thought away, like an unwanted, uninvited bird that has landed on my shoulder. It is selfish. And you are not dead. We are still here. I want to go with you, you want me to stay. You say I have much work to do. But what if this time, these days, weeks and hopefully months take all my strength away? Your sister is gentle, she glows in the light that, through the window, caresses her skin. On her first visit, she left me money. I never counted, but it felt like a lot. You told me to take it, kind gestures should not be refused. I was not happy and left it at the bottom of a drawer. In the end, we returned it, some gestures are just too big to accept. She was gracious, on both occasions. Your lovely sister with the wandering mind.

No news of your brother. Your kidney still working in a body that is breathing through a machine. You do not ask often about him. I enquire daily. Your eldest, informed by the cousins, keeps me abreast and I gauge when it is a good time to tell you. No change, no better, no worse. You know I will always tell you everything that is out of your reach. You concentrate on visitors, your guestbook, messages, and horses. I look at you from the door. There are dark patches around your eyes. You are tired but wearing your dinosaur neck with pride. Sitting upright, on your new cushion, revelling and feeling unbeatable, invincible, proud. I want to hold you, shake you, get you to eat. But this is your show, your play after all. And I busy myself with things, straightening, pondering, wiping – just for something to do. Transferring you back to the bed, now higher and fluffy, with plastic, that makes the sheets slide. You sigh, happy, contented. Sink into the gleaming white pillows, lean back, take hold of my neck, and pull me towards you. Your eyes unbroken, tired maybe, but unbroken. Still beautiful with their deceptive blue hue. Two daughters, eldest and youngest, both self-declared gatekeepers for you, tell me that they will decide who can visit and who needs to be kept away. But ultimately, my darling, I feel that it can be only you. Only you should decide, who can hold your hand, who can cry over our pillows. But the sister/cousins believe that you are too weak. Have always been weak when it comes to people. Have always given in. They say, both of them, on different occasions, that they think you are weak with me. And I, surprised, sit back, thinking of that moment, like so many others, when I am growing unsure. I ask you; I tell you that I don't want to decide. It's your show, your play, your plan. And that you have to know what is best for you. You kiss my fingers. 'Oh Queen, in the end, it has to be you. You know, you know what I need and whatever you want is good. They all know who is in charge. Me first, and then you.'

Of course, you are wrong, just another illusion, but I feel the warmth from your hand and rest.

30

Surprises

A bad night, many dreams, strange dreams. You were building a house with your brother. Big dogs in the garden and moving walls. Too many doors to escape. Whenever one door opens, a new one appears. You see your father in the garden, berating the dogs. The dogs are suddenly lions and you shoot them, one by one. It is always a big house, the one of your dreams, not always the same, often in different settings. But always large, always with too many doors. Always a garden with dark things hiding in shadows. Always stairs, too many stairs to find the right one. You had this dream for years, you say, always the same, in variations.

You, finding it hard to swallow, blinking, trying to force the water into your mouth. Retching, terrible retching all night. 'It will pass,' my beloved, 'it will pass.' I hold you, tight around your shoulders, and massage your back. Your skin, now wrinkly and thin, moves easily over your bones. I have hidden the scales, mislaid them. If you ask, I will bring them out. But if you don't see them, you might not remember. Small deceptions, I am not proud. Honesty, absolute and unfettered honesty, that was what we had promised ourselves and each other. And now, I hide things. If you ask, I will answer, honestly, truthfully, but I am trying to keep things from you. You don't know about my crying, in the car, on my own. Although sometimes you scan my face for my hidden tears. No need to cry, we are still here. We can still do things and fight. You are looking forward to today's visit. A surprise. Kate, who will be important to us soon, with her bright blue eyes and crazy love for you. And she will bring a surprise visitor. You are excited. Childlike, wondering. If they were in a box, wrapped in colourful paper, you would now shake it, examine the shape, holding them up against sunlight. But they are not in a box, and you will just have to wait. I smile, getting ready to help you across to your chair. You are not strong, but not much weaker. Not progress, but not desperate either. 27 days. I cannot decide if that is a long time, or a short interval. Tomorrow, it will be four weeks. A month. They had given us weeks and we will reach a month. And beyond. I need the beyond. I need to go on, we need to go on. For Us. I collect your youngest from Angmering station and we hurry back. I will use the time to work for an hour, get bits of food and cremes. Her glass, as always, half-empty. Strange pessimism in one so young. Me, proud of 27 days mastered and conquered, she is seeing what she thinks is to come. She looked at funeral plans, prices, and places. She wants to discuss this with you. She might do, when I am not present, but never in front of me. Later, much later, I will regret not getting involved, not listening closely. But I don't know that yet.

I leave, trying to work. Trying to make conversation with pharmacists, clients, and colleagues, and failing on every level. My mind with you – at home. Back in our space, our home, with you, I meet your visitors and I am glad. A lady who has not left her house since the first lockdown, a year or so ago. Kate brought her, beautiful Kate, who might become a friend to both of us. She loves you enough. You are happy, feel honoured and proud by the visit, and I understand why. A big decision, a great gift, to leave shielding to see someone, someone so far away at that. I love her for it and love her for the smile she brought to your face. I, who could not leave her house for three years, feel overwhelmed by the gesture. I understand more than even you. Happy and glad and scanning your face. No pain, just happy.

Suddenly, your energy leaves you, you slump a little and close your eyes. Morphine. Your breathing too fast, too painful. Maybe we have a primary lung. Kate, aware of your struggles, takes her leave. A long way, she came a long way and has a long way back. You are happy, exhausted, humbled, and loved. I am glad, I nestle my head into the crook of your arm. Not for long, it might hurt you. You guide my hand to the side of your belly. It is hot there, swollen. I sit up, need to know more. Tomorrow, we will have travelled for 28 days. Tomorrow, important, a milestone, survival past then unlikely they said. Your eyes close, I rub your swollen right side. Carefully, with oily hands. The smell of the oil soothes your breathing, and you lean back further.

'We can fight, Queen, and we will win.' I wish I could believe you. You are a conjurer, an illusionist, a joker, a flawed man with good intentions and small chances to make them work. And yet, I think, you never realised how important you are. All that supreme confidence you used to talk about, all the alpha male posturing, and in the end, you are loved. For who you are, confident, lonely, beautiful, insecure man. My husband for 79 days. I write some poems, quietly and alone, after taking your youngest back to Arundel station. I write some poems, explaining to you just how much you are. Still, you are so much. And I would still love you if you were less.

31

Loss

Today, four weeks ago, 28 days, we heard for the first time that months are not months anymore. That futures can be much shorter than 20 years. That we have to cram all our hopes, dreams, and plans into the shortest possible space. We hold each other. The morning is cold, crisp, and full of promise. All mornings should be like this. You are rested, we had only a few bathroom trips. The new medication controls the furball. Less retching, more peace, a happier face. I love you. You take my hand and give me a gift, a glis-glis no less. You tell me to take care, that the yak does not trample on it. I smile, snuggle in, sigh. Happy. We can be happy, despite all of this. Are all tumours equal? If some grow faster than others and this has been growing for years, maybe it will take a long time to destroy you completely? Or if this one is fast, was it actually there when we met? Could we have stopped it in August, September? I make coffee, hot chocolate for you. Extra cream, fortify, feed, care. You hold my arm, gently, firmly. Look up at me and I sit down. Next to you, with my coffee. 'I want us to do it again,' you say. Me, confused, stare at you. Do what? The whole 28 days? No, you want us to marry again. A few days ago, your youngest and Mr. T. exchanged vows in our room. They had planned for you to give her away. One day, during some big wedding event. But there is no time. So, they came to us, I spoke some words and declared them, entitled by no power at all, to be married. Their words to each other, beautiful and sincere. You, touched to the core. The child closest to you, the one you adored. The one you had them lock away many years before. Now a woman, a wife in the most genuine sense. You laughed and had serious talks with the groom.

You suffered when you had her committed. And yet, like always, you steeled yourself against every emotion on earth. Did what you thought was best. Had her spitting at you and biting. Saved her from herself and her thoughts. Your youngest, who, as a baby, you just could not put down. Maybe she was a new start, a new life to do better with. You are so proud of what she is now. She came through wars, many scars telling, but she is fighting to go on every day. You love her, admire her, you are proud. And when you are, so am I. Forgotten all the talk of cutting them all off at base. Teaching them lessons. And now, after witnessing this, you have decided we should do the same, on the beach. You make plans, elaborate plans. Mick being the celebrant, taking our promises. Jen and your youngest to give me away. And simultaneously filming. You have it all planned out. You will talk to Mick later. And you even set a date. The 20th or 21st, weather depending of course. I am to wear my dress again, take it out from the memory box. You might even manage your suit. It does not matter, my love, not at all. You might, you might not, it's the gesture that matters, intentions and promises to be kept. But something in me whispers and advises, to treat all this with care. Very quietly, softly, it warns me. But I don't want to listen. It will be a glorious day.

And then you receive the phone call. Not sure from whom. Your brother has taken a turn for the worse. He now has hours rather than hope. His sons, on their way to the hospital, promise to ring from his room. You will talk to your brother and hope that he hears. Your eyes broken; you lay down the phone. During the afternoon, you sit in the other room, in your kaftan, but without your neck pillow. Serious, confused, angry, sad, and alone. I cannot reach you and, giving you space, I wipe and order the kitchen, the bedroom. You speak to your brother, who cannot answer back. But the boys later tell you he smiled at the sound of your voice. You wait and during the evening you learn that your brother has gone. Stoically you just sit up. No retching. Just breathing. You ask me to be on your own. I leave you and a few minutes later you call me back and embrace me. 'It's done, now I need to give comfort. He has gone to a place of great honour. His spirit has gone far away. He is happy and honoured and will live on.' You are so certain; the words are convincing. But something in me feels the sting in your soul. Surely, you will feel the break, caused by the loss of your brother, the one closest to you. The mother of his children, gone not six months ago. When that news came, you went on the lunchtime train, to be with your brother. To comfort, to spread wisdom. You came back that night, sober and in good spirits. Talking of love and of death. Do any of us understand either? Can there be certainty, proof, of either event? But you are completely absorbed by the thoughts of giving young men hope and wisdom. They now have lost both mother and father. They have families, wives, children. They need you to assure them that things are ok, that there are better places than this to ascent to. You talk for a long time, wise, beautiful face. I hold you during the night, not moving, just stroking your shoulders. Listening to your words of peace and wisdom. And I ache for you and your brother.

32

Arabian Prince

You and your brother were close. As boys. Very close, in age and in outlook. Experiences shared; different conclusions reached. He found peace in philosophy, in his art, in himself. You painted the town in your colours, spread pain whilst looking for love. You, complex, eccentric, unpredictable, cruel at times. He, becoming a martial arts master, a Westerner held in esteem by the East, married, three boys, things went wrong, but still he remained him, unwaveringly. You loved your brother, gave him your kidney. The time in hospital the longest together in years. They were grateful, your nephews, and so was your brother. He had a chance to go to Jamaica, to see one of his sons marry. He had a few years to teach others, to become wise and serene. You saw him the last time at a funeral. The mother of his sons. He loved her, you said. Despite everything. But you also said that he was not well. You and he spoke for a long time and frankly and honestly. The two boys, who survived together, each damaged in their own way. Sitting as men and talking, both marked already, but nobody knew. Your brother's death is more than a loss, more than can be imagined.

I am worried because you give comfort to everyone but yourself. You talk of higher plains; of memorials you want to build. And all during the night, this bitterly long night, you messaged and revelled in his connections, success, and the esteem in which he was held. You are in contact with someone who was once his teacher. And you are humbled and proud, telling yourself all is good. Both you and I believe that everything happens as it must. It happens when and how it is meant to. Often, we cannot see reason in chaos, but in the end the clouds clear and we see. I hold you between bathroom trains and hot water and morphine. Your eyes fixed on the screen of your phone, trying to find words to answer. You ask about words, good words, fitting words and how they are spelled. This is hard for you, I know, but I am your eyes and your fingertips, although your fingers do all of the work. I hold you whilst you design a fitting memorial for him, your slightly younger brother. You want a bonsai, and you just know the man to ask. You want a picture and water. You can see it all in your mind. You are happy that he has ascended. Happy that he smiled at your voice. I am glad and sad and my heart aches for those two brotherly boys.

You used to go stealing with him when there was no food in the house. You two were protecting the others. Some of them went into care. They never caught you, always alert and a flexible runner. You tried to find the others and went some way to bring them home. It never happened, but you tried. You tried to protect, to make safe, to care. Your eyes bright and shining. Like in a feverish dream, you talk about seeing your brother and talking to him. Him appearing, giving you hope and grinning. I lean against your shoulder and stroke your cheek and your chin.

A cold morning, after a very long night. The kitchen floor freezing. I fill the kettle and wait. How much of your newfound wisdom is real, how long can you sustain this pain without feeling it in your bones? I will wait and watch and be ready for when the reality, the loss of your brother, really comes home to you. In these 29 days of a lifetime, we have experienced much. Hope and despair, morphine and pain, we managed it all, so far. But I don't know, I really don't know, how we are going to manage now. A quiet day, few visitors, and those who come are treated to your new monologue about death and becoming immortal, about higher places and long memories, and honour and noble pursuits. About your brother smiling at the sound of your voice and that the end is just a beginning. I hope, I so hope you truly believe all of this. Death, is it final or just a step into something else? I have no idea. We used to talk for hours on end about philosophical thought. Never really finding an answer. I don't believe in heaven and hell. Nor re-incarnation or any other noble idea. I don't know what I believe when it comes to death. Only that ours is edging closer and that there is a link between you and your brother. I am scared, so very frightened, by the thought of the After. And I hope I can stick to my word and not crumble, to keep you with me, keep you safe. I kiss you; you blink. Being strong does not come easy. Just setting one foot in front of the other. Adjusting, unwaveringly going on. But when there is nothing, during the After, I don't see myself being strong. You want me to fight with you now and alone in the After. But what will I fight for then? I have no idea what After might look like. Not even foreseeing the coming time.

You would like to have some pampering time tonight. You would like to refresh, start again, feel soft, clean, and shiny, not just a wash in bed. A bath, someone said to me long ago, is like returning to the womb. Safe, surrounded by warm liquid. You had asked some time ago for eucalyptus and I ordered oils. I run the bath, you like eucalyptus smells. Enrich the water with healing oils for your bedsores, your breathing, your skin. We make our way slowly into the steaming room. I am worried about you slipping. You laugh at my fears and trip. But we make it all the way into the tub. The room, hot and steaming, vapours that burn my nostrils, make me hold my breath. You sigh deeply and grin. I wash your back, your neck, and your legs. With fragrant coconut soap. You close your eyes, breathing deeply. The steam is clearing your chest. And after, we wrap you in soft, warm towels and oil every bit of you. Until you are gleaming, cocooned and warm, feel sated and happy and cared for. The boy in the man is at peace. You want me to take photos, I do. But when I look at them later, I gasp. My breath sticking deep in my throat. You look no longer like you. You look like a swaddled infant, or maybe some dead Arabian prince.

We lay close together for the rest of this peaceful night, under one blanket, one warmth. One safe space, just for the fragile Us. When we talk later, you say that you don't want to leave. You want to always stay with Us. And I can see your eyes sting. Not yet, my beloved, not yet, for a long time. But it tastes bitter and sad. Two years, you say, at least two years, or at least to the end of the month. You might make it to my birthday. It would matter to you. I hold you, looking at the clean, white clad you. Your beautiful ears have not changed. And I have been a wife for 80 long days.

33

Schemes

30 days, that is surely a month. A month, more than four weeks, more than they gave us. A month full of joy and tears. A month full of learning, accommodating, getting used to bathroom trains, skin that fails. A month full of learning about life and morphine, about the importance of seconds. This morning I saw your back as you tried to struggle into your kaftan unaided. The back I oil, I caress, I care for. There is nothing left now but skin. Sagging skin, not enough time to adjust to the sudden loss of your flesh. You want me to take a photo. Reluctantly, hesitating, I do. You stare at yourself. And then you tell me your mother suffocated under her skin. Her skin had become too heavy for what was underneath. It crushed her until she just could not breathe. Not for us, this will not happen to us. We have peanut butter, protein shakes, and fruit. We have 300-calorie yogurts and soups and care. You hold me, nod slowly. Your new shaver in hand, you let it glide over your head, slowly, not missing a thing.

Your beautiful face beside me, with eyes now much too large. You are wearing your glasses today, whilst studying horses for Cheltenham. You say it will start next Tuesday and you will be on top of the game. I straighten the cushions and pillows, there is really not much to say. Being next to you is a blessing, being Us is a privilege. Being whole, being home, being one after a lifetime of drifting, both of us on different paths. Gliding and sliding to this day, to this place, drawn by invisible string. I take a picture. Lying by your side, I take a picture of your beautiful eyes. You remind me, not for the first time, of a painting. It is called 'the poor poet', and I show it to you, and you laugh. You are missing the umbrella he has, but that does not matter at all.

Visitors, more visitors. This time mutual friends. They were mine once, now they are ours. They came to love you so fast. Your eldest, more quiet today, a weekend feature of sorts, feeling out of place, I can feel it. But there is nothing to do. My people, my old friends, now our friends, part of the Us, are alien to her, but she tries. Geoff, whose memory is fading. He sits quietly with us for a while. And young Eddie, my lodger once. An overexcited bee full of good intentions. And you talk about computers, technology, and your needs. I sit and prepare a lesson, enjoying the talking, the noise. Geoff tends to be grave, Eddie just mad energy. But here, in the Us, in our small world, they gleam together with you. Animated, interested, excited, you ask Eddie to build you a laptop. I frown, why another one? But you will have your reasons; you are in charge of your plans. Later you say that this new laptop will be part of the scheme you put in place to protect me from harm. You will make sure that there will be no worries at all. Not for a long time have I worried, never had much or needed a lot. I worked for what I required, worked hard, for myself, on my own. I had learned not to make my roots someone else's care.

With you, I jumped over puddles, into oceans of trust and my roots, intertwined with yours, became strong. But there is a price, there is always a price, and I might learn soon just how much I can lose. How much there will be of Nothing, during the After, the time without you, without Us. I don't want to be cared for, taken care of, looked after. I have sturdy feet and good hands. But my roots and my being are fragile without Us. And Us requires all of my strength. Eddie takes one of my laptops, the one with the virus on board. He will return it, with your new one, paid for in cash. I am thinking back, back to a time when normal was normal, and we were ok.

You had some holiday time, I had to work. You always came with me, sat in the car, playing your Pokemon. People, my colleagues, my friends were grinning. They began to expect two instead of just one. Where one went, there went the other. One waiting, the other one hurrying back. I visited 13 stations to fetch you, when you were lost, fell asleep. And you sat outside offices and houses, waiting for me. Patiently, playing and contemplating your navel. You just waited for me. And I waited for you. You suggested retiring early so that we could have more time. Me working from home. Maybe working together. More time. We do need more time, but Us now has grown finite. Time for us is running out. I hug you on our way back to the bedroom. Collect phones and laptop, water and spit bottles and cigarettes. Bring your pillow, your blanket, and rest my head next to yours. You say you need morphine; I fill the spoon. Trickly, sticky fluid spills over the rim. You open your mouth. It feels dry now most of the time. You drink oceans of water, I have a stash in the car, as well as next to the fridge. A different story with food. Less and less, more to appease me. We have stopped counting calories. I have hidden the scales more wisely. I will give them to you if you ask. But as long as you don't remember, they stay in the dark, hidden truth. Concealing what I can see. 'My empress, my life, my beautiful wife.' You sigh into my neck. I start oiling and creaming and moving your skin. Not feeling beautiful or regal, not even feeling strong. I take each of your fingers and rub in the oil. I need you to stay for a while. Absolutely and without a doubt, I need more time for the Us.

34

Balance

There are more routines now, seeped into the weeks. Not just the daily ones. The daily, hourly routines have become part of Us. The weekly repetition of visits is familiar and comforting. Mick and Jen in the afternoon, the restaurant closed. There is no more talk of walking and photo shoots on the beach. But there is serious contemplation, of your brother, the future, and Mexican food. And there are the plans for our ceremony. Hush hush between the two of you. All I have to do is iron my dress and get given away. I can do that, I think. I'm beginning to look forward to it. Jen made cake that nobody will eat. A shame, but a lovely gesture. We thank her for it. And Thursdays, Susan brings food. Cottage pie, fish pie, and chicken soup. Every Thursday and it lasts us for days, because neither of us really eat. But you say I should not stop her; it is something she can do. Feeling useful and needed. And in the end, I accept. Susan, who lives ten houses down. Opposite the second green. Susan, the mathematician, who teaches, frail and lonely, a group of wayward boys. Susan, who cooks on a Thursday, and whom you never have met. 'People need to do something,' you say, 'they are lost otherwise. Let them, it makes them feel better. They are helpless, not strong like us.' I feel differently about it, always had trouble accepting. Anything, I don't need anything that I can't do myself. But in the end, we accept, and we eat. And I learn the difference between cottage and shepherd's pie.

Late in the afternoon, just as the quiet descends, your nephews, aided by your eldest, quiet today, polite and respectful young men. All three stricken, lost in their individual ways. One blaming himself, one believing in afterlives. Another one with them, complicated and loud, pretends that the loss of his father can be managed by him, somehow. Your nephew, the son of your sister, but also a brother to you. His mother left him when he was small and helpless with your mother and your family. She never returned, apart from visits, flying in, displaying her wealth. Brothers and nephews and cousins. All broken by past and bound by present and future. He is serious, brash, loud, and considerate, all rolled into one. I sit next to you, listen, and try to lessen their grief. You hold wise speeches, to all and to one at a time. You say their father knew he was going, already at their mother's wake. You listen to them recounting last hours. You are sad with them, for them, but not yet for yourself. Your mind, stronger than ever, you console, show ways and soothe. You have the right words where I have none. I look towards my own future. When will this story be Us? It scares me, it haunts me during the nights, when there is not much to be done. They bring fish and chips and you try some. You love it and eat quite a bit. Not much by normal standards, but much for you, nevertheless. You have vinegar, ketchup, and salt. You are hungry. The hungriest you have been in days.

And I'm glad. I speak to the nephews in private. There is something grave on my mind. When the time comes, when our time comes, I would like to mingle some ashes, yours and your brothers, together again. They nod and agree. I will tell you later. They leave, with your eldest, still crying and pretending that all is well. As they leave, your nephew/brother follows me into the kitchen. His face sad, he says it feels as if you are saying goodbye. I stare back into the bedroom, and I fear I have to agree. He gives Us 72 hours. He is the half empty type. But maybe, just maybe, he might be right. 72 hours is more than 24. I take comfort in that. But as I watch, you saying good-bye to the boys and your eldest, I cannot fail to see what he sees. They leave and I busy myself, restoring order in spaces and in my head. We had more time than predicted and, really, your hunger must be a good sign at last. Surely, dead men don't eat. And then, an hour later, your face crumbles, suddenly and without warning, you scream.

There is always a price to be paid. One of your mantras of old. There is always balance and for whatever you do you will pay. Pain, there is suddenly so much pain. Not for what feels like a long time have you felt so much pain. Morphine, large spoonsful of morphine that don't even touch the sides. And after, what feels like hours, but might be minutes, or less, you lean back. Sunken eyes, blistered lips, and my hand bleeding where you squeezed it during the pain. Your mouth slightly open, searching for breath. I open the window. Cold air gushing in, reaching your lungs, but cannot ease your struggle for breath. Pain makes you breathless and scared. More panic, less air. Laws of nature invading your body. I hold you tight, cradle your head. Your breathing calms, becomes deeper. You are exhausted. And then another wave of pain. More morphine, thank God for the lack of ceiling on morphine. This time it works faster and well. For the rest of the night, we continue the dance around pain, morphine, and bathroom trains. We are not singing this time. Not enough strength and there is no tune we could hold. You, leaning heavy on me, me slowly inching the way forward over the cold floor. You supplement morphine with paracetamol. I think that a bad idea. But, ultimately, it needs to be done, we need to calm down that pain.

We cradle, we huddle, squeezing hands, doubling over, screaming, and crying. Your eyes wild. And then, just as it came, just before morning breaks, the pain stops, all gone, all quiet. You snore gently into the disarranged pillows. And all is well with the world. Wide awake, I Google some more of what livers do. And of course, they help with grease, digestion, enzymes, bile is an important factor. You cannot break down any food. And slowly, just in the morning light, it dawns on me, what this means. The pain, the hours of pain, they tell us that nothing is well. Pain is a symptom, not more and not less. It shows us that this precious liver has not much left to give anymore. That our problems are bigger and growing faster than ever. I swallow. Hard. Silently. We have had 31 days. Completed, unrepeatable past.

35

Baked Beans

Aly, the nurse, is here in the morning. She is concerned when we talk about pain. She prods a little, gently, feeling the swelling. The ever increasingly swelling just under your right rib. It is beginning to look macabre, your swollen belly against the bones of the rest that is now your body. We talk about resting your mind. Your racing thoughts and your fear. They impede your breathing, making things harder than they need to be. She suggests sedatives, you don't like the idea. 'We are fine now,' you say. I am sceptical about the 'fine' part. And we agree to accept the new pills, small blue ones apparently, as a soldier in waiting. Reserve when you feel the need. So far, CBD oil and rescue remedy have worked wonders. But maybe we need to conquer the fear to allow you to eat and to sleep. And eating and sleeping will hold you together, will help the Us to survive. I cradle your head for a while, you smile.

You have a surprise. You want to sit at the table, and you want beans on toast with some juice. Elated, I am completely elated. Practically dance through the hall. In preparation for moments like this, I bought the dinkiest, loveliest, smallest tins of baked beans and spaghetti. You used to like spaghetti on toast. Back in the cottage, for breakfast on Sunday. Rarely during the week. During the week it was liquid, coffee and one last swig. We used to wake up at five in the morning and took two hours for coffee and talking. Talking about the past, the future, the present. The ancients, the children, the cat. Our dreams and desires, dashed hopes and new plans. Of poems and pictures and boxes of wine. Of salmon shipped from Scotland to Rome, via Frankfurt and Tenerife. Of the ordinary and the miraculous. Now we talk through the nights because the days have been taken. And often we are more solemn and sad. The plans smaller, less time consuming, more urgent, more for the now. Some plans are sad, others are hopeful. You want me to take your ashes on travels all over the world. I thought my traveling days were over. But I look at my running shoes and shrug, twice. We were going to go next September. Next Christmas in Bremen, we promised ourselves. Moving for good, forever. My running shoes, twitching, warning of danger. Wanting to flee, soon, to go far away. From people, from noises, just me and your ashes. I will take you to the Valley of Kings. You will fly with the desert falcons and find a resting place in a small crack. And you will see the sun every morning, casting pyramid shadows on sand. You finish your beans, not touching the toast, you sit down on your throne and rest. I take the plate and look for the calories on the rim of the tin. Not many, a start.

On day 32, on day 83 of our marriage, I count calories in baked beans. I wonder and ponder. All of your organs are working. Your heart may be fast, but with little blue pills, under your tongue, maybe, just maybe it slows.

I have to collect them, maybe later tomorrow. The system, sometimes, is painfully slow. You still study form, Cheltenham tomorrow. I find myself humming at the cat. The cat, who sometimes did not come home for a week. Now at your feet, unwavering, unquestioning, just at your feet. He is used to the kicks, the restless nights when we push past him, time and again. He is thin, painfully thin now, showing his age. But his shout is a roar all the same. You and the cat, thin and fragile, shouting and roaring and refusing to fade. In two weekends we will have our ceremony. You are still planning and scheming. Me quietly happy and waiting, not daring to hold my breath.

I kiss you, you hold me, pull me down next to you on the chair. 'My Queen, my brave soldier, we can do anything.' I am not brave, but I will try. I will try my best, that I swear.

Your family, your youngest, one son and their mother. Just for the afternoon. You send me to pick them up from Arundel station. You feel well enough to be on your own. I tell you the brakes are not perfect, but will go nevertheless. Embraces, heartfelt and warm at the station. Nobody is saying much. Not much to say left. How many goodbyes and comforting words are left in one mouth to speak? My eyes are burning, a long day, after a longer night. Sandpaper eyelids, half closed on the road. Suddenly, unimaginably tired. Dragging myself through the afternoon. Listening to your voices, beginning to paint Easter eggs. You, smiling at me, I feel warm. Returning them to the station, I'm prickly. They say they need to be there for your dying. I promised you it would be just us. They feel that there is some unspoken rite of passage, that children must see their fathers die. I shudder, the thought of a circus, a freak show, does not appeal. Back home, I am sombre and quiet. You notice the change in my mood. I ask you about the closeness in families, more particular yours. You shrug, 'They like to think so. They like drama and big events. But close, no, never. Don't worry, my Queen, we are Us. I will protect Us from harm and bad things. And I want us to be alone.' Not sure that you will really have power, the power you think you have, I creep deep into your chest. Now smelling of oil and you.

36

Not Quite Cheltenham

This morning we thought that we'd made it. We thought it was Cheltenham week and were ready to watch the horses. Unfortunately, we are out by a week. Next week. It will be next week. I am quite content. Another week between us and a milestone. We can make it; I am sure of that. I have a little secret. A small surprise for you. The photo I took, the one you loved. Poor poet in a flat by the sea. I asked a friend to paint it. To make a picture of you. To draw you in all your beauty, and he said he will. I am excited about my plan; you feel I have something to hide. I smile and giggle a little. You will just have to wait, my darling. Just wait. You feel hot to the touch, burning. Something is not quite right. But bright and awake all the same. I wipe your face with cold, wet cloths, and you cool down. Nothing to worry about. And yet, unsettled, I watch you, unsure what this means to Us. The pain is back under control, but your belly is swelling quite visibly now. I rest my hand under your ribs, your fingers are crossing mine. I make more protein shakes, Mick recommended them. Pure peanut butter in milk and bulk oats. You gulp down the first part, smile, you enjoy the taste. But then, the little pineapple glass stands next to you for the rest of the day. I have dates, figs, grapes, blueberries, blackberries and oranges, kiwi and mango and cherries. They are all sitting next to you. I have rice, potatoes, spaghetti, baked beans, kale and spinach and beetroot and yam. The cupboards are bursting with goodness and freshness and calories. You have asked for a sandwich, so, fresh bread, butter, cucumber, posh ham and cheese are waiting for you. And yet, you find swallowing hard. Inside you, there is an appetite, you are hungry. But swallowing scares you. The furballs are back with a might. You are losing more weight, quite rapidly now. Today, you struggle to move. Uncomfortable, restless. You plan to relocate to the throne room, but as we move your legs from the bed, we realise that today we have to stay here. Today is not for moving, tomorrow, my darling, I'm sure. You drift into sleep. I am grateful. When you sleep, your breathing is fine. Not laboured, not anxious, distressed. Just oxygen entering and feeding your organs. I tiptoe into the kitchen. Floors, surfaces needing a wipe. Not enough time to replace, reorder, reshape back to the Us, what is daily, hourly trampled through. Your sister takes her seat by the bed. Never on the bed, never too close. Always respectful, always quiet and peaceful, despite the voices she hears in her head. Always uplifting, in an invisible way. I like to press my cheek against her softness and sigh. We all watch you sleep for a while. Your youngest talks about mental health, more specifically her own.

The Irish voice reports about ponds, and lining and frogs. It seems to be hard to get good strawberry plants. I nod, smile in all the right places, I hope. Your youngest and I paint at the table, whilst you peacefully snore. Not much talking required, the air is silent and thin. You move, restless, your temperature high. Paracetamol, wet cloths, and things calm down. Phone calls, you take calls and try hard to stay on topic. Still, often about your brother and heaven and new energy. I am still doubtful about your new spiritual praising of death but stay silent. It gives you comfort and makes perfect sense in a way. You speak to a man with a Scottish accent, at length, you keep calling him Irish. He lives in Ireland and you are sure. You joke, you banter, your show in full swing. You love him, his lightness of touch, his way of being honest and real compassion hidden in words. We playfully argue about his origins. I tell you he is no more Irish than I. You insist, we laugh, we will ask him next time. Running short of cigarettes and with your youngest here, I nip to the shop at the corner. The man with the sad eyes asks about you and I burst into tears. No reason for tears, really. We are still here and still strong. No pain, just a little discomfort. 33 days later, five more than the maximum time. We are still here, still breathing and laughing and talking. And you still remember my face.

37

Cells

A bad night, many of those now, growing familiar. You sleep mostly during the day. At night, things, dark things, haunt you. Shapeless and nameless, you try to explain, describe, make me see them, but words have become simple and few. The cat shouting at me for breakfast, but you are holding my arm. Tight, nearly painful, a lot of your strength still left. 'Stay, my Queen. Please stay.' You never said that before. I nestle onto your chest. Peace. Light dripping through the windows, they still need to be cleaned. And the fridge and the floors. But when? There is never a time, when you are busy, engaged without me and nobody else is around. Impossible to clean the floors and asking your mourners to lift their feet. A lot of mourning, unbearable grief from your children. But we are still here. We are still breathing. We are waiting for Cheltenham, the ceremony on the beach and straw hats, apparently. You want a party, reminiscent of Portugal. Friends, true friends around you. Energy to replenish your own. Tears weaken you, weaken us. We are weary already of grief. Not ready for it. Not yet. But they cry in the kitchen and sometimes next to our bed. And others come with the big fighting talk. The 'be strong, be brave.' They admire your show, your daily illusion, offered and proffered in videos. Complex, eccentric, beautiful prism soul. You shine and you sparkle. Lit up for others, whilst I, in a corner, polish the pieces of glass that grow dull. And hang them back where they were.

Your phone bleeps, others are also awake. Mine chimes, cockerels calling, your children. Needing answers that I do not have. The one with the worried expression asks about breathing and pulse and your weight. She never, once, asks about your mood. She asks about me, how am I doing? The answer is always the same. I don't know, I just put one foot in front of the other. No idea how I am, how I am going to be. Supportive, meaningless, empty phrases. Well meant, I have no doubt. But also confusing, demanding replies, demanding reaction without delay. If I delay, her worries grow stronger, more urgent, and then she will ring. So, my fingers respond with platitudes to empty phrases. And I wish for a coffee, made by you. I wish for us to curl up like we used to, what we used to call the best time of the day. I wish for Us, before this. Before Nothing, and morphine and steroids, before things growing in you. Before all these strangers, who are now, somehow, related to me. And I know you do, too. You, when you sigh in the evening light, 'Just us, now, Queen, just us.'

My strength is feeding us both. My care is keeping us steady. Not making worse, making safe. But will it last? I don't know. In the presence of some, I can be, just be me for a while. In the presence of others, I shrink. Shrink into the walls, the curtains, say little, smile plenty, hug and comfort. I am not pretending; I am just putting one foot in front of the other. That's what we do, you and I. Spitting and retching, you try to sit up. More pillows behind your back. I change the rugs on your side of the bed.

Phlegm does not stain, thank God. And God and I are not speaking at present. He has just closed his ears to me. Your universe, my God, one entity, have formed the unbreakable Us. Pushing us towards each other, having us forge the Us, only to take it away. This, my darling, is not difficult. Just one foot in front of the other and learn. This is not difficult, not taxing. What is difficult, is watching you disappear. Bit by bit, gram by gram. Just fading, along with your words and your spellings. Your brain still as beautiful as before. Still thinking, still planning and scheming. Still loving and silly and kind. Still cruel when you want to. Still all of your brain, but some drawers closed for good. You feel, you think, you want to express. I have to finish a sentence. You smile if I get it right. And nod. Or frown if it was not quite correct. That does not happen too often, I'm glad. God and I are not on good terms, for taking your essence away. I need justice and reason, and God just silently carries on, taking and making things grow inside.

I study cell structure and splitting. It starts slow because there are few cells. But exponentially, like R numbers, they breed rapidly. The more there are the more that can split. Compound interest for every drink. But maybe fate had this in mind, for whatever reason, anyway. Sherri drops in, she loves you. She, who hates men, has a soft spot for you. Kelly and Sherri and Jo, sitting with you and with me. Making jokes, remembering stories. The last time we met, all of us, was the first time we knew that something was coming. Something dark and unknown. We had to empty a clubhouse, take rubbish away, store things, move things and clean. We drove in silence, just holding hands. Your grip strong, but something was hanging around in the car, between us. Unspoken, your profile looked drawn. And then you tried to lift the big hammer, taking the pool table apart. I could see, Sherri could see, the shadows holding you down. Like birds carrying chains, they sat on your shoulders, weighing too heavy for you to move with the old ease. You could not breathe, could not lift your arm. You tried, tried so hard. The man, who shifted and lifted and moved boxes of wine on his own. The man who could run, but refused to, who sauntered and showed nothing but strength. You could not lift that big hammer, or the slate to set it aside. I did, trying hard not to worry. You promised Sherri to see someone. In the event it took you another two weeks to agree. In the event you, 14 days later, did finally take a Covid test. We both knew that this was not Covid, but it was something you agreed to do. Negative tests, ruling out, opening other options. At least

I could say with conviction and certainty what it was not. Another ten days and I booked something online, a doctor did ring you back. The first question, anticipated, could be dismissed out of hand. Not Covid and the doctor was glad. They advised to see your GP; I booked the appointment. And so, we stepped onto a fairground ride, increasing in speed, going faster and faster, and nobody knows when it will stop. It will stop when our tokens run out, our credit of life and of breaths. I try not to dwell, think myself back into the room.

.

38

Doughnuts

The day comes in, hazy, with various clouds, the hydrangea wavers a little, not much, no storm, no choppy sea. You, gently resting, with your head on my shoulder. Mouth slightly ajar. And I think back to the cottage, when all was hope and plans. We will have another ceremony, and you wanted another in Germany. Would I do anything different, knowing what I know now? No, I would still love you, but certainly trying to drink less and see the doctor. No longer just between you and your liver. Your liver has lost the fight. Your liver, drowned, must have grown at some point and then started to shrink. I know what the sequence is. And then, growing scars, growing angry and weak. You used to say, during last summer and autumn, that something depleted your life force, something was making you weak. I should have responded sooner, should have insisted and overruled. But I believed that you should be the ultimate judge. Free will in a person, maybe the most important thing that we have. I did not know that you were too scared, fearing the worst and avoiding it. Maybe most of us would, I don't know. You stir, open your eyes. Look at me, smile. Holding my hand, both staring at the hydrangea. It is pink in the summer; I really prefer them blue. Our first night here, in our home. Happy beyond measure. And you decided, for the first time ever, to change your address. You changed it with pride and determination. You wanted it all to be right. We stared at the sky for hours, making coffee in turn and talked.

Shortly after we moved, you returned to work. The first lockdown was over, back to the trains and the big city for you. You came back, exhausted, said you hated it now. On the train home, just after Gatwick, you started to breathe again. They changed your shifts, you had to go early. To be at the station for six in the morning, we, both bleary eyed, stumbled across to the kitchen. You no longer swigged in the mornings, just coffee with sugar for you. Now, you seldom fell asleep on the train. There were many nights before that when you overshot the station. Somehow, I always knew. Engine still running, waiting to hear your voice, three stations later, you had woken up. You hated London, the air, and the people. You did not want to go back. But the warehouse, that was important, and you were important to them. I kiss you on each eye with care. You smile. You would like to try tea. Which one? I have stocked up on all sorts, all healthy, herbal and otherwise. But you settle for builder's tea, strong and with sugar. I'm glad. Sugar is good. When people now ask you what they should bring, you ask for doughnuts. I smile. You owe me several doughnuts, from the stand at the beach. We had planned most weekends to slide over the road, walk in the sand and the pebbles, eat doughnuts and argue with seagulls. But somehow, it never happened. Somehow, we always missed the right time. So, now, people will bring them. You don't like them at all, but cut them up into pieces and try, you are doing your best. I don't like the big ones, prefer the small, crispy, and delicate ones. The ones they sell on the beach. We are grateful, however, and eat.

Susan made something with chicken, she talks in the corridor. She is still shielding and will not come into the flat. Susan, who has never met you, now catering for your palate and tries the best that she can. She wants to feed us with chicken, potatoes, and care. Kate brings a friend, and you talk. Talk for a very long time. She is watching all of your movements. Nothing escapes her, she knows. You are tired, closing your eyes more frequently now. I rush to the pharmacy and the shops, getting some bits. Random bits, but also your meds. They give me five tubes of inferior crème for the bedsore. I order crème online. It works, there is less discomfort. You are wearing your dinosaur pillow and shrink into it like a ghost. But still, you are merry, glad for the visit, the wine. Kate brings sausage rolls, the good ones, the ones that the cat likes. They leave when you can stay no longer awake. You and I manage the train and you sit down on the bed. Exhausted, but happy, nevertheless. We start the usual round of pills, dressing, and oil. Of pinpricks and soothing. Your blood clots fine, still. I am amazed, no need to apply pressure at all. I measure heartbeats and temperature and we settle, watching animals rescued until your eyes drop. But after only one hour, you are back, wide awake. We talk, we talk about your brother, his boys, and what death really means. I tell you that death is ok for the dead, hard for the living to take. I want to keep you forever. I need Us, I need peace. And you need the same, I know it. But there will be no chance of that. We have to collect minutes and seconds and keep them in precious jars. Your fingers tracing my face, soft and warm over my skin. I smile, settle onto your chest. Rest my hand on swollen enemy land. I kiss your belly, careful, you ruffle my hair. And we settle, it is nearly morning. We have had 35 days so far. An achievement, like 86 days of marriage without crossness, or anger, just love.

39

Diazepam

You have made a decision, several actually. All important in their various ways. You want to visit your mother's grave, we had spoken about that before, you wanted your mother to meet me. We had hoped for next summer, for sunshine and flowers. And a moment for you to say what you have needed to say for many years now. Then the house where you cared for your mother and lastly your sister. The hated sister, the one you call Parasite. The one who has hurt you the most. And you know who will take us, you have it already planned. And you will go to your brother's funeral, on the 9th of April. We will get there, do all of these things. I promise, I kiss you, I promise, we try. Your worried daughter, the one with a million questions, will come with her brother today. You will organise it with him, you are sure he will help. I agree, excited for you. However, your eldest has decided that I cannot be with you, at your brother's funeral, it has to be her to support, guide, and hold you upright. You are sad about that; you feel it is wrong. You will put it right. You, the emperor, the Don. You will protect your queen and yourself. I pretend that it does not matter, and really, my darling, it does not, it does not matter at all. I will wait in the car with your son. I tell your brother-nephew and he will talk to the nephews. He feels, like you, strongly, that your wife should support you and hold you and drink in your tears. He will give up his own place, so that I can be with you. I love him for this and thank him. You talk of a walking stick. You think you can manage, with me at one side,

157

and a stick on the other. You put out a message, to all of the world. And later we will drown in walking sticks. You want us to renew our vows. I also have doubts. How will we manage? How will you cope with two hours in a car? Two hours there, two hours back on both occasions. But you are excited, happy almost. You have a plan. I, in the kitchen with the chopping and blending, worry. Are you really aware just how weak you are? In the afternoon, your children, your daughter, your son, arrive. I sit with your daughter; you talk to your son. All planned, all done. You and your son tell us the plan, minutely laid out, scheduled and detailed. Your eyes shining and bright.

And then the pain is back. Terrible, horrible, skin-splitting pain. Retching to expel furballs, thinking they are the source of it all. Your belly hot, burning, swollen. Your eyes wide and wild. Screaming. Morphine. After a few minutes, you sink back; it is over, it has passed. I hold your face to my chest. I need to make a suggestion. You have fought me before over this. But as an Admiral, Queen, and Commander in Chief, I have to at least say it again. Your breathing, at night, or whenever you sleep, is calm, deep, not laboured. Your breathing becomes painful and furballs appear when you talk, worry, or try things that are now too difficult. Stress and anxiety, dangerous brothers. They speed up everything in our body, taking goodness and health in their path. We need to, somehow, calm you.

The CBD oil is no longer strong enough. And there is another, small observation. All drugs work on you for a day, maybe two. Your body absorbs, incorporates, acclimatises too quickly. What used to be useful, cherished, and healthy, has turned against you at last. You told me about three-day benders. And then 12 hours in bed, sweating it out, letting it go. And on Monday, as right as rain. But now, stress and anxiety, worry and fear, metabolism and predisposition allow the cells to grow faster. Destroy without barriers, without restrictions. In the wake of your pulse, they split like mad fleas. You listen intently and then you nod. It makes sense and we can try. I have some sedatives left in a cupboard, leftovers from a former, far away life. We try one and see. And bizarrely, strangely and quickly, there is a change. Not the one I expected. This is not expected at all. You calm and lean back, very quickly indeed. But then you are happy, chatty, and wide awake. You are witty and chirpy, record a new video for all to see. You are full of hope and need to share it. I am sitting next to you, not quite understanding what happened, but glad, nevertheless. A little, like in the beginning, before that terrible day behind the lilac curtains, I had done research, asked, found out and started giving you steroids and CBD oils. And when we shared that with the doctors, I expected them to be aghast, angry, telling us all that was wrong. Instead, they asked for the name of the steroids and prescribed them for us. 'Better to stick with what's working already,' they said, and we were surprised.

You, cheery and happy, sitting up, back to studying form and horses, me exhausted, drift off for a while. Dreaming, vividly dreaming of 86 days being your wife. Messages from your children, they need to be answered, bowed to. They need to know how you are. They ask me as well, but, as always, I do refuse to answer that part. You are doing well, there is cause for hope. Hoping for more days, hoping for calm. Hoping for quality above three. I have not forgotten that you need to reach two. If we can reach that, that magical number, we might be able to live, and you might be able to stay. For now, there is illness, pain, and discomfort. But at least there is no imminent death. That would be a five. No quality left at all.

40

Straw Hats

No pain overnight, we had some sleep. The morning is smiling, bright. We stay in bed for as long as we can. Loving watching the light. The bright light, seeping through our windows, promise of spring in the air. The windows still dirty. We lay here, just holding each other. Happy, contented, and, for a moment, we forget. I used to forget more often, now less so as time goes by. These happy moments, when fleetingly there is no cancer, and it is just you and me, without the Nothing between us. Without the pain, the pills, the measuring, the retching. Just us, laying here, breathing. Your breathing is steady, has been all night. I smile, you smile. 'My admiral, you were so right.' But nothing can last in this new world. Rest at a premium for us. Your eldest is due at ten. Getting dressed quickly, brushing my hair and then, blend, mix, fill into small jars. You now only drink through a straw. Pinprick, measuring medication. I am still hiding the scales and try not to measure blood pressure; we know it is low and your pulse is too fast. The nurse, Aly, with the soft voice and the masked face, had advised against it and now I understand why. You are examining pills before you take them, name them, part of our memory game. You recognise all of them, first time, and you still remember my face. So, I am glad, and I hold you just for a few seconds more.

You tell me about the plans for the afternoon. Four or five people with straw hats, pretending to be in Portugal. I smile, and tell you I will turn the heating up, just to keep the illusion alive. The memory of orange groves and vineyards and sun. And too much drink and the food that was cheap. Your first time away, you feel in love. There was so much travel we wanted to do. And you hold me tight in your arms. 'Next weekend, my Queen, we will go to the beach, and Mick will marry us.' I will use the time of the visit to run a couple of errands. Vitamin B and more protein water, new men pants and anything tasty to eat. It is hard now, to go to the shops. You said your eldest can learn her place and make coffee and tea and you smile; wicked, as you have won. I kiss you. Whatever I think, feel, or know, I sometimes don't approve of your methods. But they are your children and only you decide what to do. You ask for another diazepam. Too early I say, too early by far. You can have only one a day and it needs to sustain you for long. You pull a face, but are willing to wait, content with the morphine, the CBD oil. Your eldest arrives, in good spirits, making her peppermint tea. The cat scuttles out of her way. I realise, too late as usual, that I have forgotten to order my own meds. I laugh, promise not to die on you yet, set off to the shops and see James' cat. The cat is lonely, he needs some attention. I stay with him for a while. Time, finding time to get everything done. Time as a concept, time running out, time between visits. Time just for us. Time to clean fridges and floors, run to the pharmacy. Unpredictable time, nothing to waste, we don't know how much is left. I return late, everything took so much longer than planned.

People with straw hats surrounding your throne. You in good fettle, happy, animated, hold court. I love you, your beautiful face. The wit and the wisdom you spread through the room. The women, comfortable and familiar, the men a little unsure. But there are friendly greetings, hugs from those whom I know. There is love in the room, so much love and good will, my eyes sting a little with gratitude. But also, there is a small shadow, just under your eyes, dark, not rings, but blotchy and spreading. Thinking about it, rings around eyes are mostly just darkish shadows, in any shape they choose. You are tired. The fountain pen has run out of ink. I make a note to get more. They all sign the book. Your visitors' book, the thing that you never read, but that is so important to you. I must ask you later what you are planning for it. You revel, you are having a party that you just don't want to end. But you are too tired, your head falls slightly. Another party tomorrow, perhaps? Your visitors leave. You are tired and happy, exhausted, elated and sated with love. And then another ring at the doorbell. Geoff with Eddie and Debs. They bring laptops and stronger CBD oil in a syringe. Apparently, all the old people, Geoff's neighbours, cancer riddled, most of them, are happy on this one and last long. They do well on the THC. Eddie shows you for ages how everything works, setting the laptop up. Debbie, who is a bit of a healer, holding your hand, giving you some of her energy. You are taking it in, thriving and fuelling the self. Your eyes closed, feeling the heat rushing from her hand into yours. They promise to come again. Debbie's healing hands are welcome, they steady and make you happy. I hope they heal your body as well as your thoughts. They also bring a candle, you love the warm, earthy smell. And the candle has a wick made from wood, so all night it crackles and flickers and spreads its aroma, all through the protective shell.

You, who hates Christmas and birthdays and anything that requires a grateful smile. Once, for 58 or 59, you cannot remember, you thought you should do something with that day. You thought about going for dinner, a takeaway maybe or meeting some people. You were, at the time, renting a room in the house that was lived in by three of your children, their mother, and her husband. And, in the end, you spend your day, that birthday, like too many others, sitting on the edge of your bed with a bottle. Nursing the liquid and unwanted thoughts. You do not like special occasions. God knows what the boys were like. But last year, you were the first to ask to buy the Christmas tree. And of course, you want lamb for Easter.

We settle, later than usual, you have some soup before sleep. But sleep will not come, your racing thoughts keeping you wide awake. You want to make plans, want to stay with me, want everything to be alright. Like before, like it was in the cottage. But neither of us can do that. We have to set one foot in front of the other and hope that we last. We have managed for 37 days. 37 days on a ride, fast spinning, confusing, destination known but not wanted. The timetable being rewritten daily. Changing outlooks and drivers at every station.

A few months ago, you had a dream. You were on a train. Plush and somehow reminding you of the Orient Express. It was just you on the train and a man whose face was hidden. He was dressed to the nines. Velvet jacket, trousers to match and a top hat over his face. You talked, you were frightened, but you talked nevertheless. He asked you, 'Who are you?' Time and again. You grappled for answers, tried some, dismissed them and started again. And all he did was ask the same question. And you woke up in a sweat, because at the end of the dream, he took off his hat and you saw his face. And realised, it was you.

I watch your face in the light of the screen, the candles flicker some warmth at your skin. Your beautiful face, now gaunt and lost. Your cheeks no longer round and fleshy. Instead, you could be Mahatma's twin. Your Indian genes clearly visible now, a new kind of beauty. Prominent cheekbones, enormous eyes. I kiss them, these eyes, and then settle, leaning against your shoulder. Breathing in oil from your skin and the candle and fall into short-lived sleep. After 88 days of being your wife, I am tired, and worried and hopeful. Living on different levels, the past, the future, the now. Setting one foot in front of the other. Trying my very best. Nobody knows if my best is really the best for Us. You want me to protect you, but I don't know what against. I don't know if I can. But, my darling, I will, I promise, I will try my very best.

41

Tears

A bad night, little sleep, if any. You struggled to settle, to rest. Not much pain, but restless, lost, trying to keep your mind distracted. You don't want to think, you don't want to remember. Before daylight I shuffle into the kitchen, making warm water and coffee for me. You sip the warm water; I can see it soothing your throat. And then the tears start flowing. First silently, then in big gulps of gushing and gasps. You howl, you try not to stifle the pain. It has been coming for days, it is long overdue. You need to open the valves. And you cry and retch in equal measure. Me holding your shoulders, letting you sob and shake. It is good, it is right, my beloved. You cry for your brother, your mother, your life, the injustices and the pain, the lost future, the lost hopes, and your liver. You cry for every decision, every plan that went wrong. Every time you were misunderstood and every moment you pushed someone away. You cry for the children, the friends, the drinks that you should not have had. You cry inconsolably, but I will not stop you. Your cleansing is thorough. A lifetime of tears flow, over your cheeks, onto your chest and over my face. I just hold you and feel glad in a way. For you have now found the peace to empty yourself. Of all that has been and all that will never be. I think, in this moment, in the cold morning light, you are finally free to feel.

Your eldest, on a short visit, before she journeys back. Smelling of coconut oil, she talks of her children and gallstones. I have something for that, it soothes her belly, her chest. She is feeling better. You wipe your face, look strong and calm and collected. Your voice hoarse, but she does not notice, and if she does, does not say. In the afternoon, two visitors, lovely young people. They bring doughnuts because you have asked for them. The doughnuts, there is a selection, remain largely untouched. The young man, delicate of disposition, has not long since lost his mum. He struggles, as you thought he would. You give him and yourself permission to cry. The girl, wise and lovely, understands and just holds his hand. Whilst I am perching next to you on your throne, holding your shoulders, rubbing your neck. You lean your head on my shoulder, bury your nose in my hair. I have a strange sense of foreboding. Something just does not feel right. Your head is hot, too hot now. Your eyes, bright, maybe a little too bright. Your tears just keep flowing, your mouth quivers, your lips tremble. And after the visitors left, you wail, squeezing my shoulder with all your might. You say that you have tried your best, in all things, especially for your brother, and it was never enough. You could not save him, nobody could. You wanted him to live, with your kidney, do more than just buying him time. You wanted him to have 20 years, a lifetime. You feel guilty – a failure again.

Having failed everyone else. You are now afraid that you might fail me, too. I kiss you. You could never do that. You are who you are, with all your flaws and sides of the prism, but knowing that makes me rich. Richer than anything, richer than anyone could ever be. I am keeping the boy, flattering, faltering, stumbling and lonely, in my hand and hold him tight. No, you could never not be enough, more than enough for several lifetimes. But, somehow, our lifetime is short. You never felt good enough, always the failure. When we first met, you called yourself the biggest underachiever. I disagree, how do you measure achievement? And for people like us, having survived, being still here, is the greatest achievement of all. You speak to your nephews, seek reassurance that you have made some difference at least.

And you cry and you cry, until you sleep. Geoff pops in, bringing a walking stick. He sits quietly next to the bed. Holding your hand, neither of you talking. There is little or no need for words. He is quiet and you fall asleep. Still very hot, restless, shuffling your feet under your blanket, twitching your shoulders and moving your eyes in your dream. The beautiful boy in my hand, still crying, still needing protection and warmth. You always said you needed to look after your core. And now it is here, in my hand. Has been for months. And I will protect it, nurture it, love it, just for as long as I can. I will keep the boy safe, fed, and happy. But I am afraid, so terribly frightened, that you both will leave me too soon. After 89 days of marriage, after 38 days of learning and trying to keep Us alive, I am scared that, soon, there will be Nothing for me. That I might be faltering, stumbling, lose sight of the Us. That I am not strong enough to go on, not without you at least. If now, in a month or two years, you will leave me. Your body cannot sustain the growth, the dividing of cells. And what is an Us of one?

42

The Taste Teacher

After a night of endless train trips to the bathroom, bad dreams, feverish nightmares. and more and more tears, you feel tired, confused, and lost. But you try some spaghetti and toast. The toast remains untouched on the plate. Swallowing things is hard. A few weeks ago, you still liked eggs and beetroot and coffee. Now there is little or nothing you want. You drink less water, reluctant to feel anything inside your throat. It is becoming increasingly tougher to swallow your pills and your food. We lay here, entwined, you hot, far too hot. I have a surprise for you. You remember my friend with the trumpet and saxophone. He will come on Thursday, to play just for you. New Orleans Jazz, only for you. But I am not telling you yet. I have to be really sure. Sure, that you will be well enough for the music and him and staying awake. I am concerned about the heat in your body. It seems to be localised. Your belly is burning, I turn and you kiss my eyes. Tomorrow is Cheltenham and surely, we can make tomorrow. We try Aly's small blue sedative pills. You don't like how they sit under your tongue. You need to be calm, not focused on pain. You mention your medical records again. You want to see them, you want explanations, for furballs and breathing and the confusion. I ring the doctor's; a few weeks they say. Anger flashes into your eyes. A few weeks, we might not have that, and you need to know. Although, I think it is fruitless. Where is the difference in knowing? What will it change?

You retch, exhausting your muscles, stretching your chest. Your voice, now often no more than a whisper. You try to contact the hospital, the surgeon, who removed your kidney, you trust her. She was always honest, you say. She was concerned about the drink and the drugs. Told you it would come to a sticky end. She was right, of course, you now know that. But like with all mistakes, they have to be owned and dealt with, accepted and consequences have to be had. Balance. There is balance in everything. We are paying the ultimate price. Disintegrating, unravelling, shrinking life. Our life. It is not just you, paying the price. It is the Us, the unspoken, the bond and the future. You gambled and both of us lost. Did you know how high the stakes were? Did you really throw all of it in? Bulletproof Joker, with nothing to lose at the time. Death is not some romantic notion; it is not what you thought at all. Your past, you wanted to end it, you wanted out and fast. What you did not know, could not know, that you now have reason to live. A home, someone to love you and a thin, elderly cat. You now have books and paintings and friends. You have plans and a rainbow with gold at the end. And yet, nothing of that really matters. The damage is done, the game lost. Not quite, not quite yet, but already, decaying, fading, shrinking into retching and pain.

Nothing is as we hoped for, nothing is what we deserve. But everything will happen as mapped out in some bigger plan. The universe and I are at odds, and ever so often, when I leave our bubble, I scream at the wind and the sea. Your eyes, still moist and filled with sadness, tears spilling into watery rivers, dropping off the cliff of your chin. I kiss your fingers and tell you. After 39 days of fighting and learning, of making plans, we are today celebrating 90 days of me being your wife. You still, every morning, are glad that I am your wife. Say it, without fail, every morning, as soon as you open your eyes.

And so begins our daily routine of the few things we still can do. The pinprick, great values as always, the pills and the aloe vera. A yogurt, perhaps, today. Coffee for me, and more smoking. It gives me something to do, something to hold in my fingers. Last night you burned a hole in the carpet. Dropped your cigarette, as I expected and feared you would do. I laugh, cradle your face, I knew you would do this one day. And maybe one day, we will go up in flames. Maybe one day, your cigarette will fall onto your furry blanket and set us alight with a bang. I would welcome that moment. It would preserve the Us. It would spare us decisions and the unavoidable outcome, escaping on our own terms. And next weekend, on the beach, in the garden, or in this very room, we will make our vows again. You, glowing in anticipation. I wonder how much we can do. Maybe it cannot happen. You say you would kill anyone who might like to try to stop us. And for a moment, for the briefest of moments, I believe you and feel safe and held. You want to be in the throne room, to see your visitor for today. He is important to you, very important. He educated your palate, he showed you how to appreciate wine. He is young, you say, and earnest. I will collect him from Arundel. I am used to collecting people from stations, but I would rather collect you. Would rather go back to the early, chilly, unreasonable mornings and the late, dark, tyring nights. Not likely, impossible, ruled out, I sigh and set off. Leaving you, in your kaftan, with your dinosaur neck and the laptop, the phone, the tabaco, the chargers, spit bottle and water. Waiting for me to bring your teacher to you. He is not what I expected. I expected a man in a suit, with a serious face and wise demeanour. Instead, he is young, reminding me of people I used to meet on my travels. He settles into the car; I warn him of what he might find. Conversation is easy, not really a stranger. Many experiences shared, if divided by years, things seen decades apart, but still enjoyed or hated. We had felt the same wind on our skins, read some of the same books. During the short journey, the drive from the station to Us, we become friends.

He is easy to talk to, not frightened, but excited to see you. He, of all people, does not bring wine. I'm surprised. He asks for beer, and we have some, I have no idea why it is in our fridge. The fridge still needs cleaning, the windows still washing, and the floors are full of crumbs and cat hair. The sink, now a dull tea-stained colour, once polished daily, sits in accusing silence, waiting for me to do something with it. After the first lockdown, when you went back to work and I worked predictable hours, I made sure that everything gleamed, was ready and warm for you to return. Cooking at midnight was never a chore. But then, nothing with you ever was. I leave you to talk, to reminiscence and discuss philosophical issues. I busy myself, strip the bed.

I am happy, because you have a friend to cry with, a friend who can understand. On the way back to the station, he tells me his mother, a palliative nurse, has taught him to see things. And he says that things don't look good. I know this, deep down I know this. Accepting it is not the same. Palliative is another strange word. It does not mean 'end of life', it means making the unbearable into a bearable thing. Something we can carry, ease, what is going to come. 'Make easy,' mask symptoms, so that it seems as if nothing is wrong. In Latin its meaning is 'cloak'. Hiding the pain, the distress, the symptoms, to ease whatever will come. Nothing to do with palate, although they sound a little the same. We never have asked for that. We have asked for honesty, truth. We wanted to know and to see. We wanted to understand the battle. But now, I think palliative is a blessing. We have medicine to take the pain, the discomfort away. We have pills in every conceivable colour and trickly, stickly morphine in bottles. And you have me, holding your soul, drinking your tears and your fear. And we have Us, swaying between reality and illusion. Hoping, not hoping, trying to face the unknown.

43

Cheltenham

We have reached one of our milestones, our goals. Today it is finally Cheltenham. The first day; you are excited. You studied the form, although in all fairness you cannot remember a thing. You have written things down in your notepad, but in no particular order, on no particular page. Interwoven with visitors' details, missing the dates. Your breathing is laboured, more laboured than usual. I dissolve honey in hot water. Milk creates phlegm, so no more. Soft light makes your eyes shimmer, you are crying a little less. You think you would like to see an optician. You say they can tell about health through the eyes. But would that make any difference? No matter, I will find out. Jo and Sherri will take us, unless they can come here. Aly, our nurse, our ally, slightly concerned about your distress. We know, all of us, that the pain in the body is under control. The other pain, the deeper one in yourself, is bursting wide open, leaving nothing unsaid. You unburden, unpack, unload, and let out. And if I thought I knew everything, before in the cottage, in those drunken nights, I now find there is a lot left. It surges, it spits, like lava and fire, flowing all over the pillows, invading the bed. You part with memories, pain, guilt and pride, part with everything you tried to hide from the world. I kiss your eyes and hold your face in my palms. No matter, my darling, no matter at all. Hand it over to me and I will treat it with care, with love and respect. I make coffee and your hot water. You don't want to lift your cup. But you start watching the horses. I look at you from the doorway and frown.

Something not quite as it should be. I don't know what it is.

Uncertainty washes over me, like a cold wind in my back. You tell me some names of horses, I choose one; 'Put The Kettle On' is its name. Bizarrely, bitterly for you, the only one that comes in for Us. I know nothing of horses or betting. Never set foot in a betting shop. The places you hid in when you lived with your family. Coming back with nothing or tellies and toys. Always drunk, one way or the other. Always hiding away. A collection of memories, for each and every one. You hold my hand as I pass you. You are going to make sure, so sure that I will be looked after. I should not worry at all. You will buy a ten-year lottery ticket, with our numbers and they will come in. And you will win on the horses. 'Just watch, Queen, just watch.' I drink in your eyes, search in your soul. There is nothing but sincerity. Your youngest arrives, she apologises for having no money and having to take some off us. No problem at all. You send her some money; we don't need much and she has travel expenses. Your belly is hot, 40.5, your head is not far behind. I have only one lesson tonight but ask your youngest to stay. Suddenly, your head sinks to one side, you are sleepy, but different. Indifferent, resigned, not here, not really, your eyes half open, but without any sight.

Something has changed within seconds. Something I cannot explain. You have pain in your belly, a new one. You refuse to swallow, even the water is now too much. You need water, plenty of water, but you just don't care. Commentators reporting on horses, nobody listens. Horses come in or they don't, what does it matter at all? I call the nurses, unsure what this is. The fever is just too high. You say things, you mumble. Over the din of the horses, I struggle to make sense of you, of the fever, your words, and the pain. The nurses will send an ambulance. They might be some time. Meanwhile, I should use cold water to moisten your mouth and observe. I sit with my back to the bedroom, working, trying to teach. Your youngest in charge of my

Precious. My mind wanders and wonders. It is with you and not on the screen. Your youngest, her glass as always half empty, thinks the moment has come. I disagree, she rings her sister. Her sister, the worried one. The one who needs to know everything, who is anxious and nervous and wants to be useful somehow. She tells your youngest to call her again when the ambulance comes and put her on video call. She wants to observe and comment. Your youngest is angry, in tears. I end my lesson early. No point and what does it matter now? I do not know that, but this is going to be the last time I work for a while. I flip the lid of the laptop, horses fall silent at last. I embrace your youngest, calm her again. And the two people, green uniforms, efficient and calm. They examine, measure, take temperature and blood pressure. They, like me, suspect an infection, recommend hospital, tests, and blood. We shake our heads simultaneously, no prodding and pricking and hospital beds. We have decided that 40 days ago. 40 days of staying alive, defying the odds and the pain. 40 days of new programs and rules and routine. There will be no hospital, there will be no blood tests. No thin blue blankets, no nurses, no bells. There will be an out-of-hours GP. The paramedics are understanding, they do what they can for us here. And in their eyes there is respect of decisions, they don't understand, decisions that defy their training, but they do the best that they can.

In our room, in our world, you are not going to be displaced. If you want something different, we will decide again. But for now, the decision is made and is clear. Your youngest has to go home. I cannot, will not, leave you. A taxi, you say, from deep in the pillows. We will pay for a taxi to Arundel. A few days ago, you sent me out to the cashpoint, collect 'working capital' for these moments. I have been holding your card for a while. There were no secrets between us. In some ways you were more about Us than I. You gave me your bankcard, all passwords, full access. Never had any doubt. 'You are my wife.' I felt uneasy at first. Used to pay my own way, alone, without assistance. And in some ways, I am holding on. I always declined and still mostly do. You find this silly and laugh at me, but I will be learning, I am trying, I really do.

I have learned much. I have learned to read your new, sunken face. I have learned about morphine and steroids and sedatives. I kiss you and dampen your belly. The fever there raging, but the rest of you cooler, there is progress, some progress at last.

A phone call, doctors, reporting of symptoms, discussion of options. The first one is sympathetic, will send someone as soon as he can. Another one calls, the one who is meant to visit. He is not sure at all. He diagnoses Sepsis, over the phone, just like that. The only way to treat you, to maybe see you through, is the hospital now. You shake your head, adamant, we are staying at home. The doctor and I have a discussion when there is really no time to talk. He, armed with professional views and training, and Us, grappling in the dark. At last, he agrees, he will come and leave us some antibiotics. Calls it a waste of time. He arrives, a small man with dark olive skin. He opens his case and I see. A Coptic Christian, he has crosses and crucifixes next to his medicine. He examines your belly, your forehead, your eyes, and sighs. 'Maybe not sepsis,' he says. He leaves us the pills, big ones, I have to break them in half. You open your mouth and swallow. You smile and hold me tight by the hand. 'I love you, my Queen, my strong Queen, my Defender, I love you with all I am.' And there is the plan for our vows still. You are sure we will do the beach.

Outside, the weather is turning, a storm, with some rain on the way. We talk until dawn appears slowly behind the hydrangea. I drink endless coffee, more endless cigarettes, but we talk. You can find words, even if slowly. You can communicate. And you cry less. You talk of the future, surely this is just a blip. A hurdle, like so many others. I nod, I want to believe you. But all I believe, truly, is that you believe what you say. Two years, you say. We made it to Cheltenham. We will make it to April, your birthday and then mine. We will make it to summer, we will walk on the beach. Just a bump in the road. And I, holding your hand, think of one-way streets without turning circles. But every moment is good, they matter, our short moments, the time that we have to talk. Your temperature drops, and I rub your belly with more soft, cold, watery cloths.

44

Yellow Folder

Today is not a good day. Slight rain drizzles against the windows, the breeze is boring and flat. You, too tired to talk. Your voice not able to form words anymore. I hold your face in my hand. Trying to feed life through my eyes. You smile, ever so often, but then retreat again, go far away. Your forehead is cooler, your belly still burning. The only thing you swallow is water and even of that not enough. I dribble some into your mouth. You turn on the horses for betting, you still need us to make it rich. But before you can place any bets, you fall into deep sleep again. Your breathing erratic now in your sleep. I sit next to you, unsure what to do. Your soft, lovely sister comes in for an hour and we watch you sleep. Occasionally, you open your eyes, see her and smile. You know she is here. You feel protected and safe and loved. I am glad that she is holding your hand. The Irish voice tells of seed potatoes and which ones the best ones are. I strain to understand the message, but only understand every third or fourth word. They take their leave rather early; they want us to get some rest. You sleep, although it does not really feel like your usual sleep. I keep checking your temperature, your belly unbearably hot. I cool it with damp, soft, white cloths. Not sure what it means. There is the infection and that might be it. But it might be something bigger. I am just so unsure. You will not open your mouth for water and definitely will not eat.

In the late afternoon, you open your eyes. Find mine. You try to open your mouth, but no sound will come, you are mute. I remember one evening, actually late one night. You came home to the cottage, angry, upset. Shouting and beating yourself. You said that it was impossible, that nothing would work. That every time you wanted something, really wanted, desired something, it would be taken away. I sat, confused at the end of the table, not understanding a word. You had another swig from the bottle and tried to explain. The words, then, were hard to find. You knew what you felt, but it was hard to put order into the sentences, to make me understand what you said. You, over the years, had learned that not wanting was safer. Because, when you wanted, desired or longed, it would surely be taken away. And not taken away just easily, cleanly. But taken away because you were just you. Punishing you on the way. Mistakes, you made mistakes, when you thought you did right, and you paid. You paid when you stole to feed siblings, you paid when you wanted a family, you paid when your father wanted a bakery, you paid when you looked after your mother. Until you could not pay anymore. And this day, this night, this evening, you had really wanted to come home. And things conspired against you, as always, expected and so, you were late, when you had wanted to be early. You were sad. You had worked hard at not wanting anything, ever again. But we made it work, the wanting. There was no price to be paid. Not then, maybe now. We will be charged for the wanting, desire, and hoping for life.

You have not eaten all day and taken too little water. It is time for your medicine. The antibiotics, the morphine, the steroids. You must swallow them to live. But however much you want to, you can't open your mouth and swallow. There must be another way. I call the nurses, wait for them next to you, holding your hand. Kate sends a message, I tell her how hard you are trying and how little it works. The nurses arrive, ready to give you injections of morphine, antibiotics, and some sedatives. They ask me about yellow folders. I never heard of them. I collected the drugs, the pills, cremes, and injectable meds. We need a folder, to give you the medicine. There should be sheets for prescriptions, dosages visits and signatures. Without these, they cannot help us. Unless they can find a doctor, who prescribes everything yet again. I despair, you open your eyes. You see them and frown, puzzled now. I think they scare you a little, with their plastic aprons and masks. I explain and you grab hold of my hand. You try to tell me something, what it is, is a little unclear. The furball, the pain in your belly. I ask them and they have something for that. If you agree, if you give consent, they can give an injection, because this is not a controlled drug. I talk to you, try to explain. You are in and out of listening. You just hold onto my hand. Without your consent, in the absence of forms, there is nothing that can be done. I talk about furball and needles, about the chance for it to pass. And in the end, you nod. They inject you right in your belly, we wait and you sigh with relief. The nurses and I at the bedside, public space what was the most sacred of all. Your eyes open, the fever not broken, but pain subsided at last. I have to make you take your medication. If not, we have to rethink, hospitals, what is the plan, the new plan, when you cannot decide?

I try to feed you the most important antibiotics and morphine, you manage to swallow and everyone breathes again. I am glad, I am hopeful, we might be alright. I follow the nurses upstairs and I just have to ask. How to they see the prognosis? Will this see us ok for a bit? They are reluctant to answer. I rephrase the question a little. And they say it is best if I stay in my clothes. They are sure something will happen, something that might be dark. But for now, I slide next to you, in my clothes, counting your breaths and your heartbeat. I message Kate, tell her what happened. She as aghast as me. We decide to share music and candles and oils. Hundreds of miles apart, we listen to the same music. You know of my past, as I know of yours. I once was a muse, a difficult task. So, now there are pictures of me in galleries, and beautiful music to keep. You like the music written for me, many lifetimes ago, before Us. But you had moments of doubt, wondered how you could ever compete. No competition, no winner, no loser, just Us. Not even a choice, fate and destiny, determined twins, lead us together and created this Us. Thoughts wander as one. I am holding your hand, cradling your face, watching and trying to breathe life into you. And then I begin to wonder if you are not simply too weak. No food for such a long time. I go and find something to eat.

And so, for the rest of the night, listening to a piano, I feed you yogurt and cream. Spoonful by spoonful, all throughout the night. You open your mouth when the metal approaches and let the jellies and trifles glide down your throat. Until you, in the first light of the morning, open your eyes fully. You look at me and you sigh. You swallow some water, hold the bottle yourself. The furball dispersed, the pain gone. I measure the heat of your belly, much better, not normal, but lower. The colours showing slight orange, no longer angry red. I sigh, we are still here. After 41 one days of our journey, we are still here and can rest. I send a message to all the groups and the people who really do need to know. Please, you need rest, no messages, just for now. No visits, no phone calls, until you are rested and stronger. And we curl up into the pillows and watch the spring morning sky.

45

Green Bottle

Waking up after two hours' sleep, you look a little brighter. But exhausted and sleepy, nevertheless. We are still here, we are still breathing, we are still Us and alive. That counts, surely that counts. A message from your eldest, I have to sit down for a bit. I sit in the kitchen, not understanding. She says she does not believe that you are not able to answer your phone or see her, or indeed anyone. I explain, I report on every small detail. I plead with her for some time. She says she does not believe me. She will only believe what you say, not I. I sit for a while, quietly, strangely cold. My chest hurts a little, I have none of my medicine left. No matter, I go back and see you on the phone. Her in hysterics. I understand pain, I understand the desire to make you live. But you need to rest, not console, not placate, not now, please not now. You lean back in the pillows, your skin sallow and tired. Yellow around your eyes. You can no longer go to the bathroom, and I cannot carry you. We tried both. So, I empty a fabric softener bottle, the one with the widest neck. And we acquire a new skill. 93 days into our marriage, we learn to use bottles and retire the bathroom train. The fat controller no longer controlling, the carriages no longer sing. Retired, redundant for now. Instead, a sweet-smelling bottle, available on request. We are learning so many new things, so many new skills.

Your eldest messages again, angry with me, with the world. I tell her that from now on I will no longer communicate. To dismiss me like this is endangering Us. I cannot understand how, after these weeks of seeing, she still cannot understand the truth. That I care, for Us, for you, and for them. But that I must protect you, protect you at any price. If she does not value my words, take them for what they are, there is no point in me wasting them. I have few enough as it is. I am angry and tired and full of chest pain and full of worry for you. Not the best time to make decisions, but this is all I can do. I am confused, my head hurts, my heart and my body are breaking. I can no longer sustain understanding for each and everyone. And I make a final decision, about the After. My need to protect you is misunderstood. My open demeanour, my love, constructed as weakness, or meanness or both. So, I will not attend your last show, your funeral, or your wake. I cannot bear to be judged so wrongly, to be seen as something I am not. I cannot be in the same room as someone who, borne from neglect and pain, is willing to sacrifice you. They are all your children, your family, and your friends. But they can have longer, I hope, if they just allow you to rest. We are buying time, just a little more time. And I could not bear a coffin, with more than half of Us, and then watch slowly, ever so slowly, rolling away. Knowing where you are going, no, I cannot attend. I am not a natural mourner; I am private and shy. I cannot display my pain.

I stroke your cheek; ask if you can still bear it. You nod your beautiful head. We have imperceptibly, without knowing, slid down to a four. When is the quality lost? When is it really enough? What should I remember, what is really important to you? Your statements at the beginning, so warlike, so proud, so defiant, about wanting nobody to see. Or what I sense now, the desire to cram in as much as you can? Are you the same man, do you know what you want, what you need? I turn to something I know I can do and order a specially designed bottle. Green, you like green, and it will arrive here tomorrow.

Nurse Aly drops in with a folder, and yellow it is indeed. It will make things better if this should happen again. She, for the first time, just takes your hand. And then she turns slowly and strokes my cheek gently. I can see only her eyes, but I know she is sad. She is proud of what we are doing, she will support all the way, but she is sad for us, too. You sleep for most of the day, but every so often, you ask for the bottle, for drink and some jelly. Not many calories, but soothing. The furball is gone after last night's injection and you can swallow much better now. I love you more than ever, I just don't know what to do. But as the evening draws and we decide on the music, you look a little brighter. You tell people that you need time to recover, that you will try to respond, but people need patience for now. And then you ask me to assemble your office, your battle station, you want to play poker. I am pleased, happy and sure that this must be quality. This must be sufficient or even good. This must be worth having and holding. You can speak, your grip stronger. I keep feeding you jelly and trifle, and a little more crème caramel.

You fall asleep playing poker, not even leaving the virtual table. I suppose it is better than dropping your head on a real one, with real people in some pub or casino. I smile, but leave the laptop open, just in case you wake up and want to re-join. 93 days into a marriage, you still remember my face, you still remember that I am your wife. Over the past 42 days, we have learned much, lost much, grown stronger and weaker. We have learned words and how to read diagrams. We have met some incredible people and have opened old wounds to let the pain out. We tried to clean them and heal them but are not yet sure of success. I have learned to dress bedsores and massage water out of your feet. We have chosen music for long nights and short ones. Kate will listen with us again. From her living room floor, with wine on hand. She will listen and root for us.

46

Red Form

Glorious sunshine: early mornings are brighter now. Our weekend will begin soon. The weekend of vows and beach and me being given away. And yet, I am not excited. Why not? Why can I not feel the spirit of joy, expectation, and happiness? You are quiet. We have not prepared anything. We have spoken about maybe not being able to go to the beach. This upsets you; I know. But your legs do no longer carry you. Not even yards now. Something feels strange. Something feels dark, new, and unknown. 43 days of Us trying, no longer the bathroom train. The bottle arrives in the morning. You retch, extruding furballs that might not even exist. Mick will come later to finalise details, to discuss, plan, schedule. We are watching the weather, all clear, all sunshine. But there is foreboding seeping from every ounce of me. I am restless, you are retching. The bottle you say. It is green, shaped for easy use. Better than bedpans, ergonomically designed. Your thoughts wander, you try to catch them, like flies, or like moths buzzing around the room. They elude you; you have shadows around your eyes. I prick your finger, values are fine. And yet, something is wrong. I know that something has changed, I am just not sure what. And then I feel your belly, hot, terribly hot. They had said there might be infections, the antibiotics should take care of that. Three days of the antibiotics so far, three days, twice a day, part of our army. And yet. I count out your pills, there are fewer now. I have given up on Omega 3, B12, and green tea extract. I need you to swallow what is important for now. Morphine and steroids and antibiotics. Our memory test and you pass. The small pink one is morphine, a white and a brown one the steroids, and I break the antibiotics in half. You still recognise them but have to think harder.

You swallow each of them after their naming and calling them out. Less water, you seem to drink less. Your lips chapped and peeling. I use the balm Stuart has sent. Oily, sticky Australian outback balm. You like the smell on your lips. I kiss you, wipe down your face. You cry. I am glad that you allow your emotions to be. You grieve, with steady determination, for your brother, your mother, your pain, and for Us. You cry for a lifetime of not crying, not feeling, not wanting to root. You cry for despair caused by you and by others to you. You cry silently into my shoulder, my hair. 'My queen, my life, my beautiful wife.' And I cry with you, for you, for Us. For my foreboding, for all of my fears, for 43 days, nearly two months. I cry for the retching, the furballs, the ants, and the travels that will never come. We cling to each other with all the strength we have left. The morning passes, more morphine, more heat from your belly. All vitals are fine. Your blood pressure low, your pulse racing, you ask for your sedative and sleep for a while. I sit, next to you, crouched in my pillows.

I watch and try to stem that rising sense of things going wrong, of things really not going well. I feel your belly, your head. I research all possible reasons for a localised fever. I take your temperature, time and again. 36.5 on the forehead, 40.3 just under your ribs and right across the abdomen. I find something. Portal hypertension. It would make perfect sense. Low blood pressure in your body, apart from the liver connections. High blood pressure there, because it has nowhere to go. I watch and I hold your hand, not moving. I don't want to wake you. I watch your beautiful face, haggard and calm, not frightened. There is no pain. There is no discomfort. You just are so incredibly hot. You wake in the late afternoon. Smiling, you are smiling at me. You still remember my face. Kate drops in to see us. Dropping in after hours of trains and travel. She does not stay long, will return on Monday. I have asked her to write something down. Someone needs to write down your wishes, and I know it cannot be me. She does not stay long; you are sleepy and I curl up next to you. I kiss your neck and your belly. And suddenly it is no longer hot. The localised fever has broken. I laugh, the antibiotics are doing their work. I am happy, I tell you that things are ok. They will be ok from now on. You manage to stand up, go to the bathroom. We are on the train again. Fat controller attending. Slowly, we make our way. You are steady, one foot in front of the other, holding onto me tight. Me, propelling us further, further towards the bathroom, the light. I sit on the rim of the bath, as always, we talk about things to come. Suddenly you are well, so well that it scares me a bit. And then, when you wipe yourself, we both see it, at the same time, the same heart-stopping moment. Eyes wide, unblinking, we stare. Blood, a whole panful of blood. Light in colour, arterial blood. Full of oxygen that you can't spare. Not now, not ever. Some clots. Livers make clotting agents. All I can think of is red. If you are no longer clotting, if blood flows freely, it is more than just scary for Us. You need to clot; you need to stop bleeding. I lead you back to the bed. You are scared, I can see, but simultaneously well. I ring the number, they answer quickly. They require me to measure blood in cups. I have no idea, there is water in toilets, add water to blood, I just don't know. And cups come in various sizes. I personally prefer mugs. They say they will ring the ambulance; they should not be long.

Meanwhile, to keep you calm and steady, I come and sit next to you. You are chirpy, if shaken. For the first time in weeks, you feel fine. I touch your belly, look for the swelling. There is less now, much less. I see the ambulance through the window, make light, open the door. Two men, lovely, efficient, friendly, with clear questions, needing responses that are equally plain. I tell them all that there is. About your liver, stage four, terminal, weeks, Nothing that can be done. I tell them about suspected infections, fever, and swollen bellies. I tell them about sudden changes, not half an hour ago. I tell them about possible bleeding, the blood in the toilet.

They ask me again about cups. I show them the bathroom. They nod, seemingly unconcerned. I must make a decision. Soon, I will have to make a decision. About staying or going, about bleeding out or buying some days. Nothing might happen as we had planned. They take all your observational values. Blood pressure good, temperature down. Pulse normal. Everything normal – you are cured after all. And then, like a hot flush, from my toes, all my blood rushes into my ears. You want the bathroom again. And this time, with two men in attendance, there is so much more than before. We have to decide, decide now. You, upbeat, say you will go if I felt it important. You would go in the ambulance to the hospital. I nod, unable to do anything else. The paramedics make notes, are upbeat, like you. They cannot feel my blood rushing away. They think you can manage the chair, no stretcher needed, you are fairly mobile. That eases a lot of the stairs. They say we were lucky, only two ambulances working tonight. There should have been six, shortages, they tell me. And I know we are blessed. I know, in my heart, that today is not it. The grand finale – not today.

They say they will take ten minutes to strap you in and prepare. I cannot go with you, not in a pandemic. I say I will follow by car. They have doubts about me staying with you. Hospitals are dangerous places, and I might be a danger myself. I will follow them with things that we need, I will not stay away. So, I pack my rucksack. Your medications, CBD oil, rescue remedy, phone chargers, my decaf coffee, a book to read to you. Before they close the doors, you call me. You hold my hand for a second and say, 'You are so much tougher than anybody I know. I am glad that you are my wife.' I kiss you and go to the car. I know where they are going, we have agreed, and we know the hospital well. They even tell me which way they are going to go. Easy to follow, I stick to the bumper and hope that they don't shake you too much. Just before the hospital entrance, they stay on the main road, I can take a shortcut. They chose the straightest way; I am more inclined to be faster than safe and arrive minutes before you. I have told you, for the whole of our story, that I will be wherever you are. That I will be waiting, at every station, whatever the time or the distance. I will be there when you arrive. And as always over the past 18 months, I am there, when the doors open. You can see me, smile. A more watery smile now, thinner, afraid. But a smile, nevertheless. The paramedics tell me that I cannot go through these doors. That I might not be able to see you at all. Rules, they say, new rules. There is a pandemic. For me there is only one goal. I will be with you; I have to be with you. Surely, people will see that. And if not, I don't care. I dare them to tell me to wait, that I cannot be with you. Who would there be to translate? I blow you a kiss, throw you a smile, determined, make my way to reception.

A grey-faced lady, sporting an unflattering uniform and a hostile expression, warming up for Friday night. She tells me that you are not listed, not yet, and that nobody who is not a patient can get into the corridors. My eyes must tell her that she is wrong. My mouth tells her that end-of-life care trumps Covid for me every time. I say that I will go for a smoke, will be back in 10 minutes at most. And once your details are captured and the system knows you are here, I will go in there and join you. She shrinks a little way back, but still insists that the rules will not let me in. I sit in the car, illegally parked and really, I do not care. After my cigarette, I return to reception. The grey face melted and smiles an apology. She said she had tried to find me; I could go in after all. She buzzes and tells me to find you, she is not quite sure where you are. And find you I will and find you I do. Not behind paper curtains, in your own little room, labelled with some letters that make no sense to me. A nurse, her name being Joy, has already changed you into a hospital gown. You, still upbeat, smile at me. You knew I would make it somehow. You knew there would be nothing to keep Us away from Us. She has connected you to machines, back to little, bleeping red numbers. Something to focus on.

Your pulse is too fast, much too fast, your blood pressure dropping, your heartbeat uneven. I settle myself at the foot of the bed, for now. The nurse laughs with you, but her eyes are concerned. She has to take blood. I tell her your veins are shocking and she might have a bit of a job. She finds a vein, she is in, but there is no blood flowing at all. Nothing to gather, to collect for examination. She said that you are too dry at the moment, the drip should bring some fluids into your veins. I keep my eyes on the little red numbers, my ears on the bleeping and my heart in your hands. When she returns, your blood pressure is better and you bleed obediently into her phials. There are many, different sizes and volumes. As if you have any blood to spare. Your blood pressure rises, 110/76. Nearly normal, beautiful pressure. But your heart races at 144 still. Your oxygen levels are perfect, a lovely 98. Just fluids and you might be ok. You ask the nurse for a biscuit, and she is happy to feed you. A bourbon no less and some orange juice. You share your biscuits with me, when asked if I wanted a drink, I hand her my jar of coffee – yes, please, strong, just milk. I often wondered why hospitals, out of all places, do only have drinks full of caffeine. But we came prepared, so no problem at all. You want your photo taken, eating a bourbon in your hospital bed. I oblige, you laugh, I make a short video for you to share with the world. Unbeaten, not problems, a small interlude. I wish I could see it like that. Your drip is finished after an hour and within seconds your blood pressure falls, falls to unacceptable levels, 76/44. Your pulse racing faster, and faster again. You look at me, not understanding how you could suddenly feel like this.

I hold your hand, press it against my cheek. It will be fine, nothing bad here at all. The nurse brings a second drip, and everything changes again. Your eyes flicker and come to life. They move us, they want you closer to doctors and better machines. For the first time, I understand what Resas means. I follow your bed with my coffee and my Mary Poppins bag. There is a shortage of bins and I cram discarded tissues into my pockets. Retching, the retching is back for a short while, but distressing and raw. I hold your hand, standing next to you, stroking your cheeks and your eyes. Somebody brings a chair. My head leaning against the cold rails, your hand on my face and you smile. Just for a brief moment, you smile. Nurses take blood and monitor data. My eyes fixed on little red numbers and feeling your skin to gauge our truth. A doctor, young, from North London, he says, green scrubs, terrible shoes. His eyes are sincere and open. Blue, a deep and meaningful blue. He talks of bleeds, somewhere, nobody knows where. The problem is clotting and weakness and lack of blood. You have no more to spare. There might be something inside you, a tear, a small laceration. And yet, there might not. They want to see, another CT scan. He is open and honest and clear. If there is a bleed on the inside, there is nothing more they can do. They cannot investigate any further than scans. You would not live through the anaesthetic. Limited options, slim chances. But you need blood, somebody else's blood, plenty of it, to replace what you lost.

I want to ask him about cups and measuring things. But I listen, mention portal hypertension. He nods, most likely. But they don't know if your body stopped bleeding for now. He is human and honest and warm without hiding or belittling things. In his eyes I see only respect and the wish to do right by us. Suddenly, panic rising in you like the bile you can no longer produce. Rip up the red sheet, the sheet that says Don't Resuscitate. Rip it up now, I did not mean it. Panicked, you squeeze my hand. You want to live, no longer resigned to what is to come. You want to live, whatever the cost. The doctor, holding your other hand, remains calm and collected. He tells you what that would look like for you. Broken ribs on top of everything else. Probably not much brain left, and the outcome not altered at all. My eyes lock with yours, one step at the time. The sentence, past 43 days ago, still stands. 94 days into our marriage, the unaltered truth is still there. It cannot be taken away. We knew the end of our path but did not grasp the way there; were not aware of twists and turns, of things that could rupture and burst and make you bleed out. We were prepared for something, but it turns out that we really, really did not understand at all. Just one foot in front of the other.

Slowly navigating our way between thorns of pain and contortions and people to this place, to this, this, now, this ultimately truth. You scream, your hoarse voice just about reaching the ceiling. You don't want CT scans and blood. You don't want any anaesthetic because you might not come back to Us. I translate, slowly, that some things are not connected, you can have the scan and the blood. You need them and they will not hurt you. And they take you and the bed away. My chair in the room with the shiny floors makes no sense. Not related to other objects, just alone in the middle of what feels like an endless, echoing plane. When the main stage is moved, there is no fixed point, nothing to create illusions of connection and purpose. I leave, see the doctor's back. He is typing things into the system. I stand for a minute, he turns. There are tears, unfettered emotion all over his face. Respect, understanding, and love for the Us. I shudder. Remember, vaguely, something important, something I need to remember, and I cannot recall. He is going to assemble a team. Surgeons, medical and oncology, on standby, just in case they can find something they might be able to do. Not for a heartbeat did it occur to him, the possible waste of resources, of time. There are people they can save, we are not one of them. We are end-of-life care. And yet, he is determined, to give us the best, the very best they can offer. However hopeless and lost we are. He will give us whatever he can.

You need blood, you need it soon. The drips are only filling a hole. And I remember that day when, in passing, a long time ago, you mentioned your blood. How special it is. Sickle cell traits. They need to give you special blood, not just anything. More plasma, if I remember. I tell, he nods and orders more tests. I make my way to the car, still illegally parked. Sit there, holding my head, not crying, not tired. Just empty thoughts racing about getting you home again. You cannot die here, I promised. I message Sherri I think, to let them all know that we are still here, but just, only just. Back in the room with all the equipment and you return. Exhausted, empty, clinging to me. You need me, our warmth, life, and the knowledge that I will not let you die here. The doctor has found a bed on an emergency ward. He said it was tricky to allow me to stay, they are going to smuggle me in. But I have to leave in the morning, before shift changes and people ask too many questions. I have to go then and leave you here. And now I can feel our eyes sting. The doctor walks through the room, he takes my hand. Eyes locked in mine, nothing is fine, I can read it. But also respect, compassion, and the will to do whatever he can. I hope that he never loses his human face, his feeling, his warmth. We are holding hands, all of us together, a green-clad stranger and Us.

And we all understand and are working towards the one place that matters. Home. A porter, at two in the morning, takes us up to the ward. Dark, some machines bleeping, we settle, waiting for blood to arrive. More general obs, more drips, antibiotics mixed in. You need the bottle, we manage. But I shudder at the cardboard thing. Much better at home, with the smooth green one. Positively elegant in comparison. The blood arrives, I charge our phones whist you charge with blood and fluids and medication. I stroke your hand and read you another chapter of 'Once'. You, intently listening, not really hearing a word, smile, hold my hand tighter and drift off into sleep.

47

Trifles

At 6.30 in the morning, strange light, strange window, strange smells. I awake, with my face pressed firmly against the rail of your bed. Someone is calling. I must have dozed off. He is calling, 'Thomas, Thomas wake up.' My name is not Thomas, nor is yours. The surgeon, fresh on his shift, after a sloppy handover, confused your first and last name. I need some time to adjust and remember to change mine; I had promised to change my name for the very first time. But there has been no time yet. I will do it soon. Your eyes open, blood still dripping into your arm. You see me, smile, and look at the doctor. Another green uniform. Young, dark hair and dark eyes above the mask. He is cheery and bright and serious in his demeanour. He has seen the scans, the pictures of your inside. He could see no bleed, no active bleeder at least. Surely, good news at last. You are no longer bleeding. Surely, we are on our way home. He said you can have some tea now, end of the nil by mouth. My heart jumps, happy, silly little jumps. The bleeding has stopped, we are fine. A twitch, a glitch in the road. Replenished red fluids and tea to drink. And we arrange for you to come home. The surgeon's eyes rest on me. 'You need to leave, need to leave now. There will be inspections and questions and Covid. You need to leave.' I kiss you; you hold my face in your hands. I will be back to collect you; I promise, my love. I will be back and take you back to our home and the cat. To pictures and candles and music. To oil and our green pee bottle. I will be back, my love. Leaving you, in

192

your curtained room, with a nurse to attend, is harder than I could ever envisage. Impossible now, to put one foot in front of the other. The nurses smile, one shakes my hand. We are aiming to send him home, this afternoon, tonight at the latest. I leave my cardi with you, under your head. Hospital pillows, not soft and certainly not enough.

The morning is cold, neither bright nor dull. I blink for a second, my eyes not adjusting to outside and air. Making it to the car, before they issue a ticket. Leaning against the steering wheel. Making some calls, sending some messages, to let them know we still are. We are still breathing, and you will be home later. You are probably having a tea. Home, empty, and cold. Senseless without you. Lost, I wander, determined to clean to order for your return. And in the bathroom, I freeze. Blood all over the toilet, some on the floor where you walked. Honestly, I prefer blood to vomit. But yours, at this moment, is unbearably sad. I sit on the rim of the bath, unable to move. Pour bleach, flush water, but some stains remain. I never want you to see this. So, I scrub, and I clean and make good. My eyes' heavy and tired. Messages have to be sent. The middle daughter, with the worried disposition, sends endless messages, questions, supporting words. I do not have any answers. All that I have in my head – no active bleeder and you will come home. She plans to come down as soon as we're back. I am too tired to say anything. She wants to support, meaning well.

I am tired and fall onto the bed. Sleep for a fitful couple of hours. Dreams, terrible dreams. Foreboding, perhaps. But there is no bleed, so we are going to be ok. I send out messages, more messages, to keep people abreast. They return with words of hope and keep fighting. I cannot explain the dark place, the fear, the now empty space. The dread of having left you in that clinical place. Maybe the best place for you at the moment. But not the place where you want to be. Betrayed you by leaving, by taking you there. You message, despair in your words. You will have to stay after all. You will explain it all later. A few days perhaps.

I wander around the flat, our home, with the cat looking forlorn. Calling the ward, you are no longer there. They have transferred you. No longer emergency, medical now. And ironically, called Clapham. I ring the new ward, where nobody knows me. But nobody there can say yes. They can say nothing, there will be a doctor, and he will be ringing me. Leave messages, ring again and again. There is no way they are letting me in. You sleep for most of the day. I wander through rooms, thinking of cleaning, picking things up and putting them down. Pacing, ringing, your messages getting darker. You record something else for the rest of the world. Confused, and yet sounding convincing. You talk about bleeds, about winning the game. The new blood has helped your body. You look better, even close to well. And as darkness falls the first night you are not at home, I ring the ward, time and time again, only to be told that there is nobody there who can help me. Maybe tomorrow. I don't want tomorrow, I want today, I want now. We, Us, need strength, need observation, together, two heads thinking, stronger than each on their own. I go for a drive, in the darkness. A supermarket passes my way. And I buy every conceivable yogurt, trifle, and custard and some crème caramel. I buy all things easy to swallow. My phone rings, not fast enough do I answer. Trying to ring back, to be informed that this number at this time will not take incoming calls. Ringing the ward, still nobody to talk to. The nightshift cannot make decisions at all. I pace through the rooms, unable to sit or to sleep or think at all. And then you call me, 3.40 at night, howling and crying and raging. You need to be home; you need to be here. You need to be Us, you need safe and secure. Pain, you are in unspeakable but not physical pain. I watch your face on my very small screen, your eyes wide with panic at being alone. You are wearing my cardigan now. I am glad you have something that smells familiar and is keeping you warm. Exhausted, we lean back in separate places, you crying, me crying, both on our own. I want to hold you, make it all better. Ringing the ward all throughout the night.

48

PPE

Waking up in the morning after broken and painful sleep, burying my head in your pillow, soaking up smells that are no longer yours. Married 96 days. Sleeping apart for the first time in 18 months. You issue a message from your hospital bed. No visits, no calls for a while. You will stay for a few days, in that white hospital bed, surrounded by pink hospital walls. You ring me again, screaming and crying, your beautiful face contorted and wet. You have seen your brother; he wants you to calm. To get better and get back home. And finally, I get to speak to a person who knows you, has seen you, and can feel your despair. The nurse in your room, that you share with two others. Separated by curtain walls. I am not hearing her voice, hearing yours in the background and tell her I'm coming, her rules no longer apply. I tell her despair trumps Covid, mental health is health too. She waivers. I tell her, I will be there in 35 minutes. She will ring matron, she says. A few minutes later, she rings back, I am already driving at speed. Matron agreed, she says, as long as I wear PPE. No problem, I will wear nothing, or spacesuits, or whatever they want. But I will no longer, not one minute longer, wait to be with you. And so, my Mary Poppins bag and I, enter the room. Fully clad with apron and gloves. Blue gloves making it hard to wipe down your tears. You ask for the bottle again, terrible cardboard. I dispose of the gloves. How can I hold you and stroke you through strange blue plastic skin? I brought your furry blanket. You clutch it with both of your hands. Whatever happens, whatever they say, we are going home later, you are not going to stay. You cry, holding onto my hand. Kissing my fingers. 'My Queen.'

You cry silently, then sobbing, then silent again. They don't understand your pain, have prescribed the wrong dosage. I show the nurse all the pills and the morphine, all in the depths of my bag. She nods, speaks to a doctor, and ups whatever there is in the drip. There are still antibiotics in that. You are restless, I give you some CBD oil. Your stress is worse than the pain. You are sad, so incredibly sad. You cry for your brother, for you and for me, for Us and the cat. You cry and cleanse what was waiting for too many days up to now. The surgical team, three of them, knock on the paper curtain. A futile, but lovely gesture. Respect, privacy, human endeavours to make the unbearable soft. I wonder how strangers can afford us such courtesy, when your children can simply not? I sit straight, expecting the verdict that comes. There is no bleeder, no active bleed in your belly, or anywhere else. But your blood is no longer clotting. A small thing could spell a disaster. A cut, a spot, a pinprick, could make you bleed out. Not the news I was hoping for, but still. Something to remember, something learned. I ask questions, many of them. They are patient, you listen, nod every so often, with tears still streaming down your beautiful, sunken cheeks. They say there is nothing more to be done.

But that is not really news. What is news, unwelcome but not unexpected, is that there is now only the tumour, no liver left they can see. All our efforts to halt, to make safe, not worse, have done nothing, nothing at all. They disagree, they say you have done incredibly well. They mention a hospice. Now is the time to ease things for Us. We both shake our heads, like one body, one person. You will come home, whatever is coming, it will come at home, in our bed. They nod, not in agreement, but with understanding. Their eyes sad, their helpfulness useless. There will be no hospice for us. There will be no stranger you have to call and wait until they find the time. There will be no hospital bed, as much as you liked the buttons, that can make your head travel up and down. I ask what is likely to happen. They shake their heads, they don't know. There will be what they call 'an event', not specified, just an event. I ask if it will be a bleed. They said it might, but it might not. It might be something different, but surely there will be a day when the event will overtake everything else. One offers advice, useful, practical, and sensible. 'Buy dark sheets.' All our sheets are white. It will not stop whatever might happen, but it will look less bad, less dramatic. Easier to see, easier to avoid panic. Good, solid advice. We can go home; they will look after the paperwork. They will organise transport because you need to travel protected and lying down on a bed. I agree. Supporting you down our steps was something I dreaded. The nurse returns, lays her warm, gloved hand on my shoulder. She understands what we have to do.

I go for a cigarette in the car park. You send messages out on your phone. I do the same, with the phone leaning against the steering wheel. Both of us asking for peace now, no visits, limited calls. You will be in touch when you remember a person, a face, a name. You love them all. Remembering does not mean favouring. But now is the time for you to rest, to prepare, to be peaceful. We need to make time now, for Us, and collect moments. Because we don't know how many moments are left. You ask for your youngest. I call her and she says she will be on her way. She might be there before us, but no matter, she has your key and I know she will use it, whether we are there or not. Transport arrives a lot later, we have been waiting and talking. You are exhausted, impatient, and scared. But, in the end, they arrive. One of the drivers is a neighbour. Small world, incredibly small and sad. You travel slower than me, arrive later. I have prepared your bed. They help you, transfer you from the chair to the mattress. You smile, sigh, you are finally home. The three of us, your youngest and you and me. We sit in the twilight, not much to say. Holding your hands, either side.

This was the weekend of vows, of renewed promise. Of making clear to the world what we are.

And to the Us, making a gesture, a symbol, a memory. I cannot leave you, and you pay for a taxi for your youngest to go back to the station. She leaves and we hold hands for hours. No strength for words anymore. You need to rest, to try to revive whatever strength there is left. I update, let people know that you are finally home. In one piece, body intact. New blood and maybe a little more time. I ask for patience, for people to give you space. You record a message, asking for time to recuperate. No visits from now on, limited calls. Nobody left out, but not enough time to answer all messages, take all calls. You might take a few, but not all. We both stress what is important – your rest and that you will, absolutely, ask for whom you need to see. Less of a question of want now. It is only a question of need. The green bottle in constant use, you doze, cry in your sleep. You scream during one of your dreams. I hold you as tight as I dare. Sedative, morphine, calming and holding. Your eyes wild. You are reliving every second of the nightmare that was last night. Maybe we both are aware, really aware, of what is going to come, sooner than later now. I make coffee at three in the morning. Your breathing, loud and laboured next to my skin. We both feel, with all our senses, this new phase is harder than anything. We talk about the young doctor, the honest and human one. I send him some chocolates from us. And really, we were blessed to meet him. He did what he could to ease the journey and will not forget us, I'm sure. At ten in the evening, Mick airs a radio show dedicated to you. Trance, strange sounds from the laptop. You sit up, in a chair next to the bed. Proud and tired, nodding your head. Listening and being glad. Your ears waiting intently for every mention of your own name. And your face lifts, whenever you hear his voice. You hare happy, at this moment, you are happy as happy can be. I take two pictures. Beautiful you, sitting in the twilight, drifting happily to a faraway place.

The past, where everything was possible, everything a chance and a blessing. Where we could travel and you could live. At last, live and travel and soar with that beautiful mind. Sparkle and glisten, show all sides of your prism, without being ever afraid.

49

Last Words

Lack of sleep and the wounds of the weekend leave us raw, cold, and frightened. At 6.30 in the morning, you show me a message. Despair. Your eldest will come today, in the afternoon. She is not asking, she's telling. She is coming today. You are resigned, you cannot stop her. Me angry. Our message was clear. It is time for rest and for peace, you will call whomever you need. If you were to ask for anyone, the impossible, the most furthest away, I would make it happen, I would give you whatever you need. But this is against all you have asked for. We talk, you cry, you don't know how to escape, making decisions that you just cannot make. Confused, no strength left. No words to explain, again, clearer, what you need, what is really important. There are plans for today, important things you want to do. You want to see Kate to tell her your wishes. Late, but you finally have decided to write down what you want. You feel that there will be confusion or worse. Your youngest and her mother are going to visit your mother's grave. They will face-call, so that you can visit your mother. Not quite like going yourself, but lovely and thoughtful and full of meaning. These are the important things. We cling together, trying to save each other from whatever is coming our way. The Us, still intact, tries to survive before it splinters, and fragments will spill all over the sky. Your eldest will come on Thursday. You need to sleep and to rest. I kiss your eyes, tears falling. Not sure if they are yours or mine, I do not try to dry them. They leave white tracks all over your cheeks.

When Kate comes, you are still crying, for life and the loss of it. For being helpless, for being out of control. I leave the room, straighten things, talk to the cat and the wall. I do not know what is said, I will ask at a later date. However, she said you could not finish. You are tired and weepy and cannot continue after a certain point. I don't know where this point is, but I lay down with you. Kate leaves, sad, beginning to see what I see. Her back as she tackles the stairs is defeated, I can tell by the pace of her step that whatever you said, whatever she saw, will be a burden to her. Not one she resents, regrets, or wants to cut loose, but painful to carry and painful to keep. You sleep for a long time; I am not waking you up. Examining questions of duty, of love in my head. Of your rights and others. Torn, confused and alone, I try to understand and map out the best way forward for all. Whatever I do, whatever decision I make, someone will hurt, there will be pain. I can accept mine, but not yours. What are the needs of others, how far do they have a right? Your children, of course, they are your children. But how many moments, seconds, hours are needed to fill their voids? What if the balance, the eternal balance means that those moments, those seconds are lost to you, to the Us?

What if whatever you give others, is taken from your account? What if it shortens, lessens the time you have left? I cry in the kitchen, for hours it seems. But you need the bottle, the content now sticky and orange and thick. Your kidney, protesting. Organs no longer intact. Your belly, hot and swollen. Your eyes dull and dark in your skeletal face. When we are born our eyeballs are already their final size. Eyes massive in tiny faces, signalling to the world. Telling of being helpless and needing protection. Now, your face says the same. Your nephew-brother calls. I go to the kitchen to take the call. Your eldest has involved him to make sure that I know. That someone else tells me, just how wrong I am, and how cruel. And I feel cruel, I feel wrong and dirty. But I have to protect you, keep you safe and stable and calm. I tell him about the plan of your youngest. He likes it but wants to involve everyone. I tell him to call your youngest, or her mother or both. Chain reactions of hate, misunderstanding, hurt feelings. I'm lost in this endless wave of need washing over the Us. This time of dying, now a battleground for those who will live. This end of the fight or the tyring, now endlessly fought over, defaced, devalued, dishonoured. I have never tried to keep them away. I welcomed, supported, defended. Defended them against you. Acutely aware of their needs and yours, of redemption and vying for peace. Of time lost that cannot be reclaimed. Of hurt and their future. I am not protecting the Us from them, I am protecting against their needs. Their needs that will eat you, swallow you whole and are never truly filled. Your past, their past, intrinsically woven together. Entangled, cutting each other with thorns that will make everyone bleed.

You still recognise your pills; we go through them one by one. Difficult to swallow, but you succeed in the end. I feed you yogurt and trifle and sometimes some soup. You still open your mouth for the spoon. You drink water, but less now. You sleep on and off. At least I hope it is sleep. The cat lies on your left shoulder, he moves when you move or not at all. You are still in your hospital gown, no strength to change it, not yet. The face call, you stare at the screen. I can see that you grapple for feeling, you need something that is not there. You need to be there; you want to say things. Private, alone with your mother. You want to lay flowers, not have them laid for you. You need to feel the touch of the stone. A gesture, a beautiful gesture. Wasted, because nobody knew, you did not know, how important it is, this need of yours, to feel the earth of your mother's grave. To touch the stone at her head. To touch, to feel, to be one with the air that embraces you both. You need me to meet her. You cry, tears, watery and thick, streak down your cheeks and collect somewhere in the folds of your neck. Unbearable pain, unspeakable sorrow and fear. You hold my hand so tight that I cannot breathe. Too much, too much interferes, disrupts, defaces, disturbs.

Too little for you to hold onto. Too little of what you had hoped. You had hoped for peace, had hoped that redemption would buy Us the space to breathe for the last time. Together, supported and loved. But there is no redemption, no let up from past mistakes. Your daughter and son come in the late afternoon. Again, you talk to him for a while, alone, before drifting to sleep. You have asked to be taken to your mother's grave, on Thursday, as planned, as you needed and wanted. You want to be strong for the drive. His eyes are wide, wider than ever. And red and confused. He wants to go with your wishes, he wants to give you all that he can. But can he really give you this journey? Can he really be haunted forever, if something, anything, will go wrong? And it will, we all know this. I promise to talk to you later, tomorrow, or later, whenever you can. They leave, I sit here staring at you. What can I do? What can be done to give you and others the peace that everyone craves? How can I make you stronger? Your lovely, inquisitive mind is drifting, and you don't always say what you mean. You placate, you keep happy, whoever asks you can have whatever they want. Just to have peace, just to have solace. But where is your peace, where is your solace? What do you really need? Love, misunderstood, rejection, time, and harsh words, they all come back to haunt us, to hurt when no hurt can be undone. Later, days later, I am to find your last recording. Haunting and pleading for rest. But you are not strong anymore, you cannot fight for this last bit of peace and I, trying my best for the living and for you and for Us, fail you. I give in to everyone else, thinking this is what you need. I fail you; I fail Us by not being stronger. And I rest my head in your hands.

50

Yellow Cups

We wake early, there is a bit of a storm. The hydrangea shakes in the wind, and so does the lamppost behind. I like the wind and its howling. I love the sea when it's wild. Your eyes fixed on the sky. Excited. Today is a good day for you. You expect the two men, your two warehouse friends. The small Australian one and the one with the leaky eyes. Whilst we are preparing, during our daily routine, your eyes remain fixed on the window. You are waiting, so waiting for them. You listen to every engine, every car door that slams, every voice. They will be here soon, my darling. I promise, soon. I have never seen you excited like this, waiting for anyone. It gladdens my heart and yet makes me sad. They boy at last at his home. The hidden boy, the one protected by several hard outer shells. He is out in the open, sniffing the sunshine. Listening with me to the storm. Coffee and water. A little trifle, perhaps? Not trifle this morning, but crème caramel. I am happy, so happy at last. We have survived the dark hours. The damage done by being apart is slowly receding. Healing. You're healing again.

Your beautiful mind wanders, it wants to make plans, wants to make sure. You anticipate something, apart from the visit. The weekend, your brother still fresh in your bones. Whilst I make the coffee, you send me a message. I frown for a moment, but smile. 'Loving you is so therapeutic; I just cannot get enough.' Now, sometimes, speaking is harder than typing. Words are differently formed. I look at your face and I wonder; one side of your mouth appears to be lower. Maybe a trick of the light. Maybe your cheekbones cast shadows. Create illusions of things that are not really there. I kiss you, massage your skin with the oil. You can't take your eyes off the window. Your ears straining for sound. My mind wanders back over the weeks. Glad, knowing that we made more than a month. We had Cheltenham and doughnuts, we had trains and bottles. We have been able to manage. We will continue to manage. We will have April at least. We will have the sunshine and pink hydrangeas, and rain and we will visit the sheep. You look at the picture, drawn from a photo. Proud and happy. Steve brought it to you last night. Steve, who never goes out, who avoids the pandemic, stays at home, and paints pictures of India. He came over all this way. Just dropping the package by. Not staying, not having coffee or talking. Just handed me the flat parcel and left. I let you open it and you gleamed. I took a picture of you looking at yourself. More like the poor poet than ever. 'The boss,' it says, 'Like a boss.' I framed your likeness. And we found a spot where you could always see it. My beautiful poet, glancing through glasses, at the eternal Us.

They arrive, a little while later. You hear a car door and smile. You are sure that they have arrived. I doubt it, a van, not a car. But your senses were right. They sit next to you, next to the bed. The wine shimmers in glasses. Your wine untouched but poured into your special one.

The three of you talk, slowly, but happy, about nothing of note. About life, your brother, and wine and cheese. I sit with you for a while. Then run some errands, giving you space and me time to collect more medicine. When I return, you are sleeping. They watch you with sorrowful eyes. They look at me and I look at them and there is something new in the air. So, we sit for what seems forever, just watching you sleep and stir. You are dreaming away the weekend, the time away from the Us. It has shocked you and hurt you, being so utterly lost and alone. But, my darling, you are home now and safe and warm. Your sister and the Irish gardener arrive a little later. Now five people are watching over your sleep. You stir gently, open your eyes. Smile brightly and wide and content. Your sister brought yellow cups, one for you, one for me. I embrace her. You never can have enough cups. Your friends take their leave, a long journey back. I walk with them up the stairs. Drinking in the air from the sea, I hug them for one last time. I tell them that I would like to share the After with them when it comes. I would like to spend your funeral day in the warehouse with people who love you, nearly as much as me. They nod, gravely, and understand. I think something was said. You might have spoken whilst I was away. They don't tell but nod all the same. Yes, that would be lovely. That would be a great plan, indeed. And both of them promise to come back again. We all know how unlikely that is. They tell me to stay in touch, whenever. Stay friends even after the After. I believe them and hope for the best. The bond between us might not be there for much longer. Although I will do what I can. We smile, hug again, and they leave.

I return to our room. To our bubble of love and safety, to everything that is good. You, sleeping again, your sister now holding your hand. We smile, make some conversation. But really, there is not much to say. There is love in the room, for you and for Us and everyone else cocooned by these walls. They leave. I am the only one watching you sleep. And then you stir and start retching. Retching like never before. Unstoppable, cramping retching, wide eyed, panicked, tearing and searing pain. I call the nurses. They have to come soon. There is not much more you can take. You writhe, there is phlegm all over the carpet and bile, for the first time – bile. The nurses arrive, efficient and calm. They know what to do when I don't. I kiss you and hold you and cradle your face. They have an injection. It will make this pain go away. A new one, something that cannot be swallowed. Controlled, but it works, every time. You ease yourself back. Eyes empty. It has passed, for now anyway. They say it will buy us hours, maybe a night without pain. I think, wrongly as it turns out, that you having bile is a good sign. Surely, something is working inside?

They look at me with some pity, but also compassion and calm. I can ring them again, anytime, if I need to. I will and I don't see them out. However, the small, dark one, turns back. She offers night watchers and carers, but carers would require a hospital bed. I shake my head. No strangers. We have had enough of that. Staying with you, holding your head. Holding the Us to be safe. You rest for a while, in deep sleep. How will I be able to know the difference between sleep and the moment you go? Will I know, will I understand? Will I be able to give you permission to leave when you need it? Will I be able to hold you for long enough to know? For now, I am holding your face and your head. You rest for most of the night. Sleeping, calmly, no retching. Just the green bottle. Urine now sticky and orange. Darker with every time. I know that your kidney is failing. Would you be better with two? Fluid, you need fluid. I spend the night, syringing water into your mouth. You, grateful, taking it in. Thirsty. Your lips chapped and bleeding. More water, more life, more time.

51

Mischief

You wake up early in the morning, you feel well, you feel better. No extra morphine needed. No pain anywhere. I am slightly confused. How can this thing, growing in you, now greater than everything else, how can it suddenly stop hurting? Where is it gone, the pain? And then I remember, decades ago. Seen this before, just with more distance and clearer. I shudder, I don't want to remember. Surely, I must be wrong. No pain, anywhere in your body. I massage your skin, dress your sore. You smile, you are actually laughing. 'Mischief,' you say 'today is a good day and I will cause mischief. Just watch, my Queen, just watch and see.' How much mischief will you be able to make from your bed? I have no idea. But it makes me happy. Your smile makes me happy and hopeful. We might have turned the corner; the infection might have gone away. And we will be able to have more weeks, months even, or years. We are talking about the future, the glorious future ahead. No pain, absolutely no pain anywhere. Your youngest arrives with her partner. You told them to take a taxi from Arundel station. I am no longer to leave your side. They arrive, I pay for the fare. She is loud and brash, and he plays on his phone. You struggle to breathe, and your words are sparse. But your eyes shine brightly. Your beautiful eyes say it all. You are better, I know it, a lot better, I can see. Your youngest takes me to the kitchen. She talks about funeral plans and the After. I don't want to hear any of it. She talks about what will happen and that your children must all be here. I

208

shake my head, you had told them that that was no option at all. Just Us, you and me, nobody else. She talks about feeling pushed out. I leave her in our kitchen. I want to be with you. Your beautiful face is shining. No pain. For the first time in weeks – no pain. We talk about your eldest, scheduled in for tomorrow. It will do you no good, but I cannot change it. She is your child after all. You don't mention the planned outing. We have never mentioned our ceremony that was not. We sit with you for a while. You play poker and sleep. Equal measure in time. I am sure, you're not winning and smile. They leave, they have things to do. I pay for the taxi back. We sit for a while, next to each other. You chuckle and hold my hand. 'My Queen, my warrior Queen. We are doing so well after all.' I kiss you and hope that tomorrow will not be a trauma too far. As you drift into sleep, a stranger appears, bearing a Zimmer frame. The plan was to adjust it, so that you can walk on your own. She looks at the bed, at you and your body. Decides that between us, we can adjust the height. We estimate, try, and she shows me the buttons to make things right.

During the night, I feed you trifle and jelly and crème caramel. And suddenly, you turn your head. Away from the spoon, away from me. And tears stream from those beautiful eyes. Large tears and you sob. 'I am so sorry; I am letting you down.' And I know – no more from now on. I will no longer try to feed you, will not fill the spoon again. I will just drip water and the wonderful hydrating cream we took from the ward. I cry, I feel guilty. I should have noticed. I should have noticed that you are tired, done, all in for your part. Whenever your phone makes a noise, your face crumbles and you try to push it away. In the end, I put it into your drawer and let the battery run its course. I have always told you that when the time comes, I will stop. You will let me know, you promised. You promised me many things. After 99 days of being your wife, I should have noticed it more.

52

49 days

And after day 49 – forty-nine days, nearly down to the hour, seven weeks since diagnosis, four months into our marriage, I am no longer a wife. I am a widow. Me, torn, left over, rejected, howling with a voice that is not my own. Us is broken, no longer, unfixable, gone. I hear the howling, the breaking humanity in someone's voice. The animal tortured, freed, and lost. There is nobody here but me. I am trying to catch you, to feel you, to find you. But in the end, there is Nothing. You left and my soul has left with you, and I can find neither you nor me. I will remember that moment forever. With me, encased like in amber, that last bit of pulse that just stopped. Trying to keep you warm. Making two calls, one of them a mistake. Regret, deep regret – I should not have called them. I felt they needed to know, your children, your family. Mistake, I should have kept you. For a little, for the remnant of Us. They had come in the afternoon. After all that pain, after all that searching for ways to accommodate, placate, understand, trying to protect them and you and Us, they came that afternoon.

In the morning, you were no longer able to speak. Not sure if you were in that body at all. The body, suddenly discharging fluids and matter all over the bed. Cleaning you up, looking to comfort Us, I looked at your face, and there was nothing. No involvement at all. Not even stoic acceptance. It is what it is. A man at the door tried to deliver a mattress. Better defence against bedsores, aiding my dressing and cleaning and turning you over. I stared at him, blank, unseeing, and suddenly my eyes flooded. He, bewildered, stretched out his hand towards me. No mattress, please, I know there will be no need. But maybe there will. Making decisions, impossible. I cannot make any decisions now. Unsettle things where there is no conceivable good. He left, internally shaking his head. His shoulders spelling confusion. Mad woman. Soon to be widowed. But he could not know that and nor did I. I changed the sheets, with you in the bed. You could not help anymore. You, frustrated that you had lost your words, tried to communicate something, unclear, unknown, movement of lips and jaw, but despite my ear leaning next to them, I could not understand. I understood water and holding. Your face already the shape of a skull. I kissed it, watched for the frown. Your frown replaced words and found meaning. Communication by skin. You stared passed me, towards the doorway and smiled. Your beautiful smile, old smile, mischievous, wistful, bitter, and sweet. Anticipating, seeing, welcoming. I asked if you saw something, someone. You wrinkled your forehead, agreement.

Your brother, you saw your brother and I did not. I did not see or feel anything you could feel then. Just cleaning the vessel that had been you. And holding and dripping water into your cheeks. The small things, you had learned to love small things. Now drops of water are bigger than skies and mountains and seas. I held you, just held you, preventing atoms and cells to flee. Calling the nurses. The pain will come, and I need them to bring and administer medicine before it takes hold. Before it surfaces. I will not tolerate pain. They came with their needles, sharp boxes, and masks. I have never seen the whole of their faces. They speak with their eyes, calming. You speak with your eyes, pleading. What do you want me to do? I stub my toe on the commode, parked in the hallway, where we used to be a train. Your youngest, the eldest boy, and middle daughter appear. I knew they were coming. Did not anticipate the sudden rush of air, traveling through the opening door. Your middle daughter, with her nervous disposition, her worry, her need to help, crumbles. Why did you not tell me? Why did you not tell me how bad it is? I shrugged, confused, lonely, without being able to reach her skin. I shrugged because there was no answer. One foot in front of the other. No longer smiling but breathing and oiling and choosing music to calm your soul.

She sobbed, broke into small atoms, right on the chair that was yours. They sat with you, your daughters. They held your hands and whispered. You could not reply, but you knew they were there. I am sure you knew they were there. Your son, caged animal, raw with red eyes. Twisting his fingers, wandered from room to room. More boxes arriving, dark sheets. Recommended by nurses with training and skills and experience. Dark sheets make things look less dramatic. Reduce trauma for all concerned. The nurses and your daughter helped me to clean you, the bed, replace sheets. Clever ways of moving your body. They know – I do not. They are gentle, experienced, brisk, and up to the task. I watched, in awe. Efficient, with purpose and skill. I froze. Craving coffee and wanting to vomit. Shaking. Your eyes on me. But you did not see. You had already left. I am sure of that. You, as I know you, part of Us, no longer existed. Maybe you went with your unseen brother. You left no message for me. Your skin, still warm, smelling of oil. Penetrated by needles that brought you calm and ease breathing, we hoped. Today was the day when, with an elaborate plan, your eldest was going to say her goodbye. I was going to leave, no longer able to bear her presence, frightened I would say terrible things. True things, but hurtful, nevertheless. I was going to leave, Jen letting them in, your middle and eldest daughter. Me meeting Jen at the beach, to return an hour later. How many goodbyes does a person need? How much is needed only to find that some things cannot be ended, fixed, finalised, cleaned? But I was not going to deny this. I could not, should not, would not. In the end, you cancelled the visit. The elaborate plan left redundant.

Like many plans I had made. Stonehenge, the falcons, the trumpet. Failed, redundant, to be forgotten, filed as overly and unnecessarily ambitious. Your breathing a problem, rattling, white fluid collected in the back of your throat. And when they left with their embraces and assurance of family and that they cared, cared for me because I cared for you, it was just Us. Your eyes broken. The music, medieval harp, calming the senses. Easing whatever is yet to come. Medicine flowing into your arm from the box the nurses fitted earlier in the day. I am holding your hand, kissing your shoulder. Your breath rattles, but less I believe. No pain, I know there is no pain. Your forehead and your skin tell me that. Your skin, smooth as always, too big for your body, but still your skin. I rub oil into your right arm, slowly, gently, pressing lightly on every pore. No noise, suddenly there is no noise. I look up. You stopped breathing. Your pulse shows strongly on the side of your neck. Paralysed, I watch as you catch your breath, deep, wholesome breath, filling your lungs with air. No rattling, no furball, no white, foamy fluid. I lean my face against yours. I want you to hear me, wherever you are.

'Just go. If this is too much, just go. There is a storm over the water, and you can fly away on its strength.' And you stop breathing again, not looking at me or anything else. Just stop for what seems like hours. Only to breathe deeply and long. I kiss you, feel myself crying, I should not cry when you see. I am not sad; I don't want to be sad. I want you to stay and tell you to go. I want to go back seven weeks, eight weeks, a year. I want to go back to Us, to the ancients, the plans, the virtual presents, entwined in each other. I need to go back. You stop breathing again. I watch the last bit of pulse at the side of your neck. No dramatic, big gestures, no soul flying away. Nothing. Prosaic. And I know. And before I break completely, I make two phone-calls. One to the nurses. The other one a mistake. They come back, your children, into my screams and your cooling skin. They come back with their noise and fresh air. The girls try to dress you, make you comfortable, presentable. The youngest rings the undertaker. No answer. Maybe people don't die at night. I don't know of any. Maybe of one. I had seen a sign, opposite the station, next to my friend's house. I tell her the name. She finds the number, I think. Your daughters are tender with you, make you comfortable, all seems to be right as it is. I lie next to you, keep you warm. They order pizza and wings. They cry and they are practical, efficient, comforting in their industriousness.

From nowhere, Mick appears. I don't know who called him and why. He takes me away from your body. For a few minutes, we sit in the other room. I think I am talking, describing, taking him with me through Our journey of a few hours ago. I need to keep you warm, that is all I know now. As long as you are warm, you might be able to hold my hand, look at me, say something of substance. But your skin is cold, and your bones stiffen. I am lying there, adding more covers. More and more covers and the warmth of my body. The nurses come, very late. I know one of them, she is small, human, efficient and kind. I know her, she knows me, she is holding my hand for a while. She says there is no pain in your face, no anguish, no stress. And that I did my best. All I could do; all we could do. That we had much longer than anyone hoped. They leave, leaving papers behind. Important, I will need them. Later, much later, or maybe now. Your youngest stands at the foot of the bed, talking to your middle daughter, across my cradling arms. Relaying a message from an old lover. The one whose name is tattooed on your hand. They talk about her and you. I open my eyes. I ask if she was pretty, the answer is not what I want. Her name on your skin will go with you soon, my wedding ring will not. Metal does not burn, skin does. The pizza box on the table, plates on the floor, the cat opening a carton of wings and distributes bones evenly on the floor. They have left. Just Mick and me. Mick in the other room, me holding you.

Thinking about your tattoo, about your skin, about you having said nothing. No words to record. No last declaration of love. Trying to keep you warm, so that you might open your eyes.

I am your wife, we are One, we are Us, but you have left and I have to be me, when I have no idea how to be that anymore. When they come to take you away, I sit in the other room, stroking the cat, staring at pizza boxes and glasses. Dead flowers, books without meaning. They tell Mick that your youngest is down as your next of kin. He tells me and I nod. Unseeing, unhearing, unfeeling, just cold. After you've gone, I bury myself in your pillow. To stay forever in this space, curled up, smelling the last bits of Us. I stare at the dead tree, lonely and left, alone and cold. And you, lonely and cold, somewhere else, without me, without Us. I have been part of Us for 18 months, your wife for 100 days. Train driver without training, nurse without skills, drug expert without expertise, learner of dressings and loss, cook, chopper, dresser, driver, and hostess, admiral, queen, empress for 49 days. Now all of them without a post and purpose. And what I don't know yet, what is still to come, is to find that the nature of tortured, resentful, and lonely people, the nature of need and misunderstanding, of the prosaic and hungry, will cancel all that is beautiful, moral, and just. And ultimately, that I am not as strong as you thought and that I will fail you and Us. And that really, my darling, we did not matter at all.

53

Epilogue

So, after our journey of 49 days, there is no longer an Us. There is no longer the sanctuary of hope and of milestones and things I can do. I can no longer pretend to be useful. Before you, I was Me, then I became part of Us, and now I am Nothing, nothing at all anymore. Your children, true to their nature, think they are in charge. You were their father, and that was all that there was. My father, my Dad. They are allowed to grieve. I am standing alone, blinking into the sunshine, outside for the first time in nearly two months. Outside with no need to come back. Really outside, no hurry, no shopping to do. Just me, alone in the sunshine on the steps to the sea. And I flee back. Inside is safer, or maybe not safe at all. 19 hours after your death, your youngest, hard voice on the phone. She demands that I cash in your pension. The funeral more than she thought. I need to get money so that they can have your funeral. In style, as befitting their father. With words written in flowers, at £50 a letter for small. I suggest smaller, she calls it a pauper's deal. She never returns your phone, uses it to access all areas of your, our life. Meddles and changes, because she is your daughter. Blood, they tell me, blood is what counts. And hundreds of other small wounds they cut deep into already weak flesh. Occasionally I bite back. But there are so many of them, and there is just me. I will not attend your funeral and I might not get your ashes. They take your rings off you and hand them to their mother. I am, after all, not blood. I am nothing. Don't matter at all. Edited out, erased, withered into the heap of pebbles that was once your memory and ours. Some of them have nice words, but I know they are not reaching their eyes. Platitudes, 'I know you are grieving'. I know that I am hard to look after, I might even be hard to love. I am prickly and lonely, strange, sarcastic, I want people and I need to be alone. I need someone to hold me together before I entirely disintegrate, explode, implode, become nothing but a collection of atoms, losing their speed and can't bond. I push people away, well-meaning people, I pretend that I'm not at home. I shut out and reach out, all in the same sentence. I know I am hard to love.

Your family, they publish a piece, according to which you died, peacefully, contented amongst the people you loved the most – your children. They want your things, your phone, your belongings, your money, your body, your ashes. I am not blood and only blood counts. They don't remember the fighting amongst them. Their fear about me pushing them out. The trouble with you, my beloved, is that as your beautiful prism, you only ever showed sides. You showed every person who came into your orbit the side they needed to see.

So, everyone knew a different version of You. But with Us, in Us, you were able to be, the whole, the round sphere, that sparkled and shone and cried and failed and was a complete man. I miss you; I have lost you. No smell can bring you back. I need to know that you loved me, that all of this was as it just had to be. That, had you lived a little while longer, you would have put protection around me. That maybe, what's happening now, can only happen because you did not have time. I miss you; I love you. I doubt you and Us. Our beautiful dream. I doubt that we ever happened. But I promised to write you down. All of you, warts and all. And on this day, irony of all ironies, your medical records arrive and your new men nappies; I leave them outside in the hall. In the kitchen, the peanut butter, the shakes, the trifles, and crème caramels stand and accuse me of having failed you. And in your last days, I learned to roll cigarettes, you were impressed, so was I. And next to my pillow, the last half you left. The one you were going to smoke later. I will keep that, your mother's cross, and your dressing gown. The rest, in the end, are just things. And I will keep the treasure we found together, for absolutely no reason at all.

I promised to put you on paper, to hold you deep in my heart. I have not changed the sheets. The same that saw your soul flying away. The fighting begins, they never return your phone or your wedding rings and we argue about the ashes. In me, there is nothing but pain, screams, and nothing. I am hoping this nothing will kill me as well. Lying in the dark, in our sheets, just about feeding the cat. And after a week or ten days, one merging into the other, I finally have a bath.

Printed in Great Britain
by Amazon

65528698R00132